Fundamentals of Statistics: Concepts and Applications

Dr. Santoshi Kumari

Assistant Professor

Mathematics

Center for Distance and Online Education

Chandigarh University, Mohali, Punjab

Preface

Statistics, as a field of study, serves as a cornerstone in a variety of academic disciplines, providing essential tools for analyzing, interpreting, and drawing conclusions from data. This book is designed to introduce readers to the fundamental concepts, techniques, and applications of statistics, with the aim of helping both beginners and those with prior knowledge in the subject develop a deeper understanding.

The first chapter provides a comprehensive introduction to statistics, offering clear definitions from prominent scholars like A.L. Bowley, Croxton and Cowden, and Horace Secrist. It goes on to explore the various types of statistics and discusses its evolving scope and significance in a rapidly changing world.

In subsequent chapters, the book delves into essential topics such as frequency distributions, measures of central tendency and dispersion, skewness, kurtosis, correlation, and regression analysis. Each topic is addressed systematically, with detailed explanations and numerous examples that allow readers to grasp both the theory and practical aspects of the subject.

Chapter 2, on frequency distributions, explores different ways of organizing data, including raw, discrete, and continuous data, as well as the construction of frequency tables and various types of frequency distributions. Through clear examples and step-by-step instructions, the chapter enables readers to create their own frequency distributions and interpret the corresponding graphs.

The discussion of measures of central tendency in Chapter 3 offers insights into different methods of summarizing data, including the mean, median, mode, and geometric and harmonic means. The book also addresses the merits and limitations of each method, empowering readers to choose the appropriate measure for different data sets.

Chapter 4 introduces measures of dispersion, exploring techniques such as range, quartile deviation, mean deviation, and standard deviation, all of which help quantify the variability within a data set. The chapter also includes practical examples and exercises to reinforce the concepts.

In Chapter 5, the concepts of skewness and kurtosis are introduced, with a focus on understanding the symmetry and the shape of data distributions. The chapter covers various methods for measuring these characteristics and explains their relevance in statistical analysis.

Chapters 6 and 7 tackle correlation and regression analysis, two powerful tools for understanding relationships between variables. These chapters provide in-depth coverage of the various types of correlation and regression, along with formulas, assumptions, and real-world applications.

This book is intended for students, researchers, and professionals looking to build a strong foundation in statistics. It emphasizes the importance of a conceptual understanding of statistical methods, accompanied by practical examples, exercises, and solutions that reinforce learning. Whether you're just beginning your study of statistics or seeking to refine your skills, this book will serve as an invaluable resource.

I hope that this text serves as a helpful guide and encourages a deeper appreciation for the power and applicability of statistics in solving real-world problems.

Dr Santoshi Kumari

Assistant Professor of Mathematics

Center for Distance and Online Education

Chandigarh University, Mohali, Punjab

CONTENTS

Chapter 1: What is Statistics, Basic Concept, Scope of Statistics

1.1: What is Statistics, Definition?

Statistics is a scientific discipline that focuses on gathering, organizing, summarizing, and analyzing data in order to make generalizations about the entire population (Winters R et al., 2010). The Latin term "status," which means "a (political) state," seems to be the source of the English word "statistics." When statistics first started out, they were just data on various facets of people's lives that the state might exploit (Asthana H.S et al. 2007). But throughout time, its focus widened, and statistics started to focus on more than just gathering and presenting data—it now involved interpreting and extrapolating conclusions from the data. The gathering, organizing, analyzing, and interpreting of data are all aspects of statistics. The term "statistics" might indicate several things depending on the situation. Observe the sentences that follow:

1. Please provide me with the most recent edition of "Educational Statistics of India."
2. I enjoy studying "statistics" because it's a useful subject in daily life.

1.1.1 Definitions by A.L. Bowley:

Statistics are numerical statement of facts in any department of   enquiry placed in relation to each other.

Statistics may be called the science of counting in one of the departments due to Bowley, obviously this is an incomplete definition as it considers only the aspect of collection and ignores other aspects such as analysis, presentation and interpretation (Gelman et al., 2013).

Bowley gives another definition for statistics, which states 'statistics may be rightly called the scheme of averages' . This definition is also incomplete, as averages play an important role in understanding and comparing data and statistics provide more measures (Gupta, S.C. 1990).

1.1.2 Definition by Croxton and Cowden:

Statistics may be defined as the science of collection, presentation analysis and interpretation of numerical data from the logical analysis. It is clear that the definition of statistics by Croxton and Cowden is the most scientific and realistic one(Gupta, S.C. 1990).

1.1.3 Definition by Horace Secrist:

Statistics may be defined as the aggregate of facts affected to a marked extent by multiplicity of causes, numerically expressed, enumerated or estimated according to a reasonable standard of accuracy, collected in a systematic manner, for a predetermined purpose and placedin relation to each other.

1.2 Types of Statistics

Although many bases have been used to categorize statistics, the two main approaches are (i) function-based classification and (ii) distribution-based classification.

1.2.1 On the Basis of Functions

Three types of statistics have been described since statistics involves specific processes to deal with its data or subject matter.

Descriptive statistics
Descriptive statistics is the field that deals with descriptions of the data that has been acquired. A specific population category is defined for corresponding features based on these descriptions (Efron et al., 1994). Classification and tabulation measurements of central tendency and variability are included in the descriptive statistics. These metrics make it easier for researchers to describe the phenomenon by allowing them to understand the trend of the data or scores (B.L.Aggrawal 2009).

Correlational statistics: These statistics reveal the relationships between the collected data. It covers a wide range of methods for calculating data correlations. Additionally, correlational statistics give a description of the population or sample for subsequent analysis to determine the importance of the differences.

Inferential statistics: These statistics deal with making inferences about a big population or group of people based on the observations of a small number of participants or on occurrences that are yet to happen based on previous occurrences. It offers instruments for calculating the likelihood of the participants' future behaviour.

1.3 On the Basis of Distribution of Data
The two categories of statistics based on data distribution are parametric and nonparametric (Tukey et al., 1977). Both are also focused on the sample or population. The total number of objects in a sphere is referred to as its population. Generally speaking, it has unlimited number therein, yet in statistics, a population's number is finite, such as the number of college students. "The term population and universe mean all the members of any well-defined class of people, events, or objects," according to Hively (1968). Three general types of qualities can be found in statistical populations: (a) having a finite number of items and being knowable, (b) having a finite number of articles but being unknown, and (c) maintaining an infinite number of articles.

1.3.1 Sample is referred to as a portion of the population that embodies the characteristics of that specific population. The sample selection will be more representative of the population even though it will be impartial and random. "A sample is a portion of a population chosen (often in accordance with a process and with a specific goal in mind) that is thought to be representative of the population as a whole."

1.3.2 Parametric Statistics
According to parametric statistics, the population being studied is assumed to have a normal distribution. The term "parametric statistics" describes statistical methods that were created presuming a particular kind of data. Specifically, the score should be derived from a normal distribution and the measure should be an interval scale.
Nevertheless, despite the parametric statistics' many benefits, certain drawbacks have also been identified. It further restricts the range of its application and is obligated to adhere to the strict assumption of normal distribution. When the sample size is tiny, parametric statistics cannot be applied since a normal distribution cannot be reached. Furthermore, due to huge samples and

numerical computations, parametric statistics computation is time-consuming and intricate. Among the main parametric statistics used for data analysis are the T-test, F-test, and r-test (Ziliak, et al., 2008).

1.3.3 Nonparametric Statistics that do not assume a normal population distribution are known as nonparametric statistics. As a result, another name for these is distribution-free statistics. They don't have to be utilized with an interval scale. Data is regularly distributed. These statistics should be used to deal with non-continuous data. Nonparametric statistics are employed for analysis of samples in which the assumption of a normal distribution is not easily maintained. Due to the lack of a normal distribution, nonparametric statistics are applied to samples containing few elements. In addition to ordinal data, it can also be applied to nominal data. Chi square, the Mann-Whitney U test, Kendall's rank difference method, Spearman's rank difference method of correlation, and others are examples of common nonparametric statistics.

1.4 Scope of Statistics

Developing effective methods for processing, analyzing, and deriving reliable conclusions from numerical data is what statistics is all about, not just gathering data. Every aspect of human endeavor, both social and physical, uses statistics, including biology, Information technology, business management, planning, education, and commerce, among other areas. Finding a single area of human endeavor where statistics cannot be used is nearly impossible. We now quickly go over how statistics are used in various fields (Stigler et al. 1986).

Policy planning: In order to finalize a policy, certain information from the past or anticipated environment is needed to ensure that the policy may be used efficiently and yield the greatest number of positive outcomes. For instance, an organization's historical sales data are examined in order to create future tactics in the industry that will maximize product sales.

Management: Statistics are a highly helpful tool in an organization to assess different areas of work and employee well-being as well as to monitor the organization's progress trend.

Business: Demand forecasts, product pricing tactics, and market segmentation all make use of statistical techniques. Organizations can increase profitability and streamline operations with the use of tools like time series forecasting and regression analysis (Hastie et al., 2009).

Healthcare: Clinical trials, epidemiology studies, and public health research all heavily rely on statistical methods. They guarantee that healthcare policies are grounded in evidence and assist in assessing the efficacy of interventions (Freedman et al., 2007).

Engineering: Statistical techniques are applied in engineering to process optimization, reliability analysis, and quality control. To improve production processes, methods such as design of experiments (DOE) are crucial (Agresti, 2018).

Social Sciences: To examine survey data, gauge public opinion, and measure the effects of social policy, social researchers employ statistical techniques. Strong study of social patterns and human behavior is made possible by these techniques (Stigler, 1986).

1.5 Evolution of Statistical Methods

The development of statistical techniques is firmly anchored in human history and scientific advancement, mirroring the growing demand for data analysis and interpretation. The evolution of these techniques has been influenced by developments in computational technology, probability theory, and mathematics.

Early Foundations

1. John Graunt (17th century): Frequently regarded as the father of demography, Graunt established the foundation for contemporary statistics by applying statistical analysis to population data. Patterns of births, deaths, and illnesses in London were studied in his ground breaking study, Natural and Political Observations Made upon the Bills of Mortality (Stigler, 1986).

2. Carl Friedrich Gauss and Pierre-Simon Laplace (18th century): These mathematicians had a key role in the introduction of ideas such as the normal distribution and the development of probability theory. Strong instruments for data analysis and prediction were made possible by Gauss's contributions to error theory and Laplace's work on the method of least squares (Hald, 2003).

1.6 Conclusion

The science of gathering, organizing, evaluating, and interpreting data in order to make defensible conclusions is known as statistics. Since its inception, it has served a variety of industries, including business, healthcare, engineering, and the social sciences, in addition to state administration. Descriptive, correlational, and inferential statistics, together with parametric and nonparametric techniques, are important categories (Winters R, et al., 2010). The wide-ranging nature of the topic facilitates decision-making in scientific research, management, and policy development. Its evolution was aided by pioneers such as Gauss, Laplace, and John Graunt. Despite developments in data science and technology, statistics is still crucial for resolving challenging real-world issues.

Chapter 2: Frequency Distribution – Table, Graphs, Formula

A statistical tool called frequency distribution aids in both organizing data and drawing insightful conclusions. It indicates the frequency of occurrence of any given value in the dataset. Data is arranged using a frequency distribution in tabular form, which displays the frequencies (the frequency at which values occur) in a dataset.

A frequency distribution shows the pattern of how often a variable's values occur in a dataset. It displays the quantity of instances for every value that could exist in the dataset (Gravetter FJ et al.2000).

2.1 What is Frequency Distribution in Statistics?
In statistics, frequency distribution gives the number of times (frequency) that different values are dispersed across a specified time period or interval in a table, list, or graphical   representation.
A frequency distribution is an overview of all values of some variable and the number of times they occur. It tells us how frequencies are distributed over the values. That is how many values lie between different intervals. They give us an idea about the range where most values fall and the ranges where values are scarce (Gravetter FJ et al.2000).
Frequency distributions come in two varieties: grouped and ungrouped. To be helpful, data— which is a collection of numbers or values—must be arranged. Let's examine the frequency distribution of the data.
 2.1.1 Data
Data is any bit of information that may be represented as a value or number. Data includes things like the amount of cars that cross a bridge in a day and the grades you received on your math test. In essence, data is a compilation of facts, measurements, or observations.
2.1.2 Raw data
A first collection of information is known as raw data. There is currently no organization to this data. You will obtain raw data following the initial stage of data gathering. For instance, we ask five friends in a group what colour they like most. Blue, Green, Blue, Red, and Red are the responses. The raw data is this compilation of facts.
2.1.3 Discrete and Continuous Data
There are continuous data and discrete data. Discrete data is information that is expressed as whole numbers, such as the number of tigers in a zoo or the number of students at a school. It can't be in fractions or decimals. Continuous data can be in decimals instead of whole numbers. A week's worth of city temperatures, your percentage of final exam scores, etc. are examples.
2.1.4 Data Collection
There are two methods for collection of data Primary and Secondary Data
These are data that an investigator gathers for the first time with a specific goal in mind. Since primary data are original and have not undergone statistical processing, they are considered "pure." The Indian Census serves as an illustration of primary data. Whereas the data that have been gathered from an original source. This indicates that some researchers or investigators have already gathered this type of data in the past, and it is available in both published and unpublished form. Since they may have previously undergone statistical processing, this data is tainted. Information

from the Department of Finance's website, the Government of India, or other repositories, books, journals, etc., serve as examples.

2.2 Frequency Distribution Table

A table in statistics that lists all of the values and frequencies of various things. A large amount of data may be efficiently recorded and retrieved using this method. It facilitates simple data visualization according to frequency, which essentially indicates how frequently a given piece of data occurs.

One method for organizing and presenting data in a tabular format that aids in condensing a vast dataset into a manageable table is a frequency distribution table. One of the two columns in the frequency distribution table displays the frequency of each interval or individual, while the other column displays the data in the form of a range or a single data set (Dawan B et al.2004)

"Frequency" refers to how frequently an event occurs. For example, the frequency is 72, which is the number of times your heart beats in a minute, if your regular heartbeat is 72 beats per minute.

For instance, Rahul rolls a die several times and records the following results: 4, 6, 1, 2, 2, 5, 6, 6, 5, 4, 2, 3. She uses tally marks in a frequency distribution table to group the numbers (1, 2, 3, 4, 5, 6) into groups so that you can see how frequently each one occurs.

Outcomes	Tally	Frequency
1	|	1
2	|||	3
3	|	1
4	||	2
5	||	2
6	|||	3

Example: Draw the frequency distribution table for the following data:
2, 3, 1, 4, 2, 2, 3, 1, 4, 4, 4, 2, 2, 2
Solution: Since there are only very few distinct values in the series, we will plot the ungrouped frequency distribution.

Value	Frequency
1	2
2	6
3	2
4	4
Total	14

2.3 Types of Frequency Distributions

There are Six types of frequency distributions (Swinscow, T. D et al.2003):
1. Exclusive Series

2. Inclusive Series
3. Ungrouped frequency distributions
4. Grouped frequency distributions
5. Relative frequency distributions
6. Cumulative frequency distributions

2.3.1 Exclusive Series: The term "exclusive series" refers to a series with class intervals in which any item with a range from the lower limit to the value slightly below its upper limit is included. Because the frequencies corresponding to the particular class interval do not include the value of its upper limit, this type of frequency distribution is called an exclusive series.

For example, if a class interval is 0-10, and the values of the given series are 4, 10, 2, 15, 8, and 9, then only 4, 2, 8, and 9 will be included in the 0-10 class interval. 10 and 15 will be included in the next class interval, i.e., 10-20. Also, the upper limit of a class interval is the lower limit of the next class interval.

Age	Frequency
0-10	5
10-20	2
20-30	8
30-40	1
40-50	4
50-60	6
	Total=26

From the above table of exclusive series, it can be seen that the upper limits of the first class interval is the lower limit of the second class interval, and so on. Also, as discussed above, if the data includes a value 10, it will be included in the class interval 10-20, not in 0-10.

2.3.2 Inclusive Series: Inclusive series are those that have class intervals and include all things with a range from the lower limit to the upper limit. The higher limit of one class interval does not repeat as the lower limit of the subsequent class interval, similar to exclusive series. As a result, the upper-class limit of one class interval and the lower limit of the subsequent class interval are separated by a gap (0.1 to 1).

For example, class intervals of an inclusive series can be, 0-9, 10-19, 20-29, 30-39, and so on. In this case, the gap between the upper limit of one class interval and the lower limit of the next class interval is 1, and the class intervals do not overlap with each other like in an exclusive series. Statistical analysis with inclusive series might be challenging at times. The inclusive series is changed to an exclusive series in specific circumstances.

Marks	Frequency
10-19	2

20-29	8
30-39	3
40-49	5
50-59	6
60-69	6
	Total=30

From the above table of inclusive series, it can be seen that the upper limit of one class interval (say, 9 of interval 0-9) is not the same as the lower limit of the next class interval (10 of interval 10-19). Also, all the values that come under 0-9, including 0 and 9 are included in the frequency against 0-9.

2.3.2.1 Conversion of Inclusive Series into Exclusive Series

The inclusive series may occasionally need to be converted into exclusive series for statistical computation. Assume that in the scenario above, some students had scores of 10.5, 40, 5, etc. In this instance, the series will be transformed into an exclusive one.

An inclusive series can be turned into an exclusive series by following these steps:

Determine the difference between one class interval's higher limit and the subsequent class interval's lower limit in this initial phase. Subsequently, the difference is divided by two, and the resultant value is added to the upper limit of each class interval and subtracted from the lower limit.

Example: The inclusive series of the above example is converted into exclusive series as under.

Marks	Frequency
9.5-19.5	2
19.5-29.5	8
29.5-39.5	3
39.5-49.5	5
49.5-59.5	6
59.5-69.5	6
	Total=30

2.3.2.2 Difference between Inclusive and Exclusive Series

The upper limit of one class interval in an inclusive series differs from the lower limit of the subsequent class interval. The difference between the upper class limit of one class interval and the lower class limit of the subsequent class interval ranges from 0.1 to 1.0. The upper limit of one class interval, however, is equal to the lower limit of the subsequent class interval in the Exclusive Series.

The value of the upper and lower limits are only included in that class interval when it comes to inclusive series. The value of the upper limit of a class interval is included in the subsequent class interval rather than in the class interval itself in the case of Exclusive Series.

An investigator can only use Inclusive Series if the value is in whole numbers rather than decimal. Nonetheless, an investigator can use an Exclusive Series regardless of whether the value is in decimal or whole numbers.

Only once it has been converted to an Exclusive Series can it be counted in Inclusive Series. Nonetheless, it is always feasible to count in Exclusive Series.

2.3.3 Ungrouped frequency distributions: The quantity of observations for every variable value. This kind of frequency distribution can be used to categorical variables.

2.3.3.1 How to make an ungrouped frequency table

1. Make a table with two columns and as many rows as the variable's values. Write the variable name in the first column and "Frequency" in the second. Put the numbers in the first column.

- The values in the table rows for ordinal variables should be arranged from least to largest.
- The values of nominal variables may appear in the table in any order. You could want to arrange them logically, like alphabetically.

2. The frequencies are counted. Each value's frequency indicates how frequently it happens. Next to their respective values, enter the frequencies in the table's second column. Tallying the frequencies may be helpful, particularly if your dataset is vast. Include a third column with the name "Tally." Mark each observation with a checkmark in the corresponding row of the tally column as you read it. To find the frequency, count the tally marks.

2.3.3.2 Example: Making an ungrouped frequency table

A gardener set up a bird feeder in their backyard. To help them decide how much and what type of birdseed to buy, they decide to record the bird species that visit their feeder. Over the course of one morning, the following birds visit their feeder:

Ungrouped frequency table of the frequency of bird species at a bird feeder

Bird Species	Tally	Frequency
Chickadee	|||	3
Dove			1
Finch	||||	4
Grackle	||	2
Sparrow	||||	4
Starling	||	2

2.3.4 Grouped frequency distributions: The number of observations for each variable's class interval. Class intervals are arranged groups of values for a variable. For quantitative variables, this kind of frequency distribution might be applied.

2.3.4.1 How to make a grouped frequency table
1. Divide the variable into class intervals: One way to split a variable into class intervals is shown below. There is no consensus on the most effective way to determine class intervals, but different approaches will produce different results.
- Calculate the range: Deduct the dataset's lowest value from its highest.
- Decide the class interval width: Although there are no hard and fast guidelines for selecting the width, the following formula serves as a general guideline:

$$\text{Width} = \frac{Range}{\sqrt{sample\ size}}$$

This value can be rounded to a whole number or a suitable addition number (such a multiple of 10).
- Calculate the class intervals: There is a lower limit and an upper limit for every interval. Within a class interval, observations fall below the upper limit and exceed or equal the lower limit:

$$lower\ limit \leq x < upper\ limit$$

The dataset's lowest value is the lower limit of the first interval. To determine the first interval's upper limit and the second variable's lower limit, add the class interval width. To compute more class intervals, keep increasing the interval width until you surpass the maximum value.
2. Create a table: with as many rows as there are class intervals and two columns. Put the variable name in the first column and "Frequency" in the second. In the first column, type the class intervals.
3. Count the frequencies: The number of observations in each class interval is known as the frequency. If you find it useful, you can count by tallying. Next to the respective class intervals, enter the frequencies in the second column of the table.

2.3.4.2 Example: Grouped frequency distribution
A sociologist conducted a survey of 20 adults. She wants to report the frequency distribution of the ages of the survey respondents. The respondents were the following ages in years:
52, 34, 32, 29, 63, 40, 46, 54, 36, 36, 24, 19, 45, 20, 28, 29, 38, 33, 49, 37
Solution: Range = highest -lowest
Range = 63-19
Range = 44

$$\text{Width} = \frac{Range}{\sqrt{sample\ size}}$$
$$\text{Width} = \frac{44}{\sqrt{20}}$$

Width = 9.84
Round the class interval width to 10.
The class intervals are $19 \leq a < 29$, $29 \leq a < 39$, $39 \leq a < 49$, $49 \leq a < 59$, and $59 \leq a < 69$.

Grouped Frequency table of the ages of survey participants

Age, a (years)	Frequency
$19 \leq a < 29$	4
$29 \leq a < 39$	9
$39 \leq a < 49$	3
$49 \leq a < 59$	3
$19 \leq a < 69$	1

Example: Make the Frequency Distribution Table for the ungrouped data given as follows: 23, 27, 21, 14, 43, 37, 38, 41, 55, 11, 35, 15, 21, 24, 57, 35, 29, 10, 39, 42, 27, 17, 45, 52, 31, 36, 39, 38, 43, 46, 32, 37, 25

Solution: As there are observations in between 10 and 57, we can choose class intervals as 10-20, 20-30, 30-40, 40-50, and 50-60. In these class intervals all the observations are covered and for each interval there are different frequency which we can count for each interval.

Thus, the Frequency Distribution Table for the given data is as follows:

Class interval	Frequency
10-20	5
20-30	8
30-40	12
40-50	6
50-60	3

2.3.5 Relative frequency distributions: The percentage of observations of a variable's values or class intervals. When comparing frequencies rather than the total number of observations is more important to you, you can use this kind of frequency distribution for any kind of variable.

2.3.5.1 How to make a relative frequency table
1. Create an ungrouped or grouped frequency table.
2. Add a third column to the table for the relative frequencies: Divide each frequency by the sample size to get the relative frequencies. The total of the frequencies is the sample size.

$$Relative\ frequency = \frac{=\ (Frequency\ of\ Event)}{(Total\ Number\ of\ Events)}$$

2.3.5.2 Example: Relative frequency distribution

Bird Species	Frequency	Relative Frequency
Chickadee	3	$=\dfrac{3}{(3+1+4+2+4+2)}=0.19$
Dove	1	.06
Finch	4	.25
Grackle	2	.13
Sparrow	4	.25
Starling	2	.13

From this table, the gardener can make observations, such as that 19% of the bird feeder visits were from chickadees and 25% were from finches.

2.3.6 Cumulative frequency distributions: The total of all the frequencies from earlier values or intervals up to the present one is known as the cumulative frequency. Cumulative frequency distributions are those that use cumulative frequencies to illustrate frequency distributions. For ordinal or quantitative variables, this kind of frequency distribution can be used to determine the frequency with which observations fall below particular values.

There are two types of cumulative frequency distributions:

Less than Type: We sum all the frequencies before the current interval.

More than Type: We sum all the frequencies after the current interval.

2.3.6.1 Cumulative Frequency Curve: Let's look at a grouped frequency distribution that is provided. Take a graph paper and write the matching cumulative frequencies along the y-axis and the upper-class limits along the x-axis. These locations can be joined repeatedly by smooth curves to create a curve that is referred to as the cumulative frequency curve. Or to put it another way, a cumulative frequency curve is a graphical depiction of the cumulative frequency distribution. Also referred to as ogive, it is the most effective method of data representation. Cumulative frequency curves come in two varieties:

2.3.6.2 How to make a cumulative frequency table

1. Create an ungrouped or grouped frequency table: for a quantitative or ordinal variable. Since there is no order to the values—one value is neither greater nor less than another—cumulative frequencies are illogical for nominal variables.

2. Add a third column to the table for the cumulative frequencies: The number of observations that are less than or equal to a specific value or class interval is known as the cumulative frequency. Add each frequency to the frequencies in the preceding rows to determine the relative frequencies.

3. Optional: To determine the cumulative relative frequency, divide each cumulative frequency by the sample size in a new column.

2.3.6.3 Example: Less than cumulative frequency distribution

Age, a (years)	Frequency	Cumulative frequency	Cumulative relative frequency
$19 \leq a < 29$	4	4	4/20=0.2
$29 \leq a < 39$	9	9+4=13	0.65
$39 \leq a < 49$	3	9+4 +3=16	0.8
$49 \leq a < 59$	3	19	0.95
$19 \leq a < 69$	1	20	1

From this table, the sociologist can make observations such as 13 respondents (65%) were under 39 years old, and 16 respondents (80%) were under 49 years old.

2.3.6.4 Less than cumulative frequency curve

Interval	Frequency
5-10	2
10-15	4
15-20	5

By summing all of the prior frequencies up to the current frequency, we will determine that the intervals and frequencies in the above table are less than the cumulative frequency.

Interval	Frequency	cumulative frequency	Lower Limit
5-10	2	2	10
10-15	4	2+4=6	15
15-20	5	6+5=11	20

2.3.6.5 How to draw less than cumulative frequency curve:

In this instance, the curve is drawn using the classes' upper limit. Here is the detailed procedure for creating a frequency curve that is smaller than cumulative:

    1. Mark the matching cumulative frequencies along the y-axis and the upper-class limits along the x-axis on a graph paper.

    2. By joining these locations one after the other using line segments, we can create a polygon called a cumulative frequency polygon.

3. A curve known as a cumulative frequency graph is created by joining these spots one after the other with a smooth curve.

4. Cut the above curve at point P by drawing AP ‖ x-axis from a point A (0, N/2) on the y-axis. Cut the x-axis at M after drawing PM ⊥ to it.

5. Next, OM's median length.

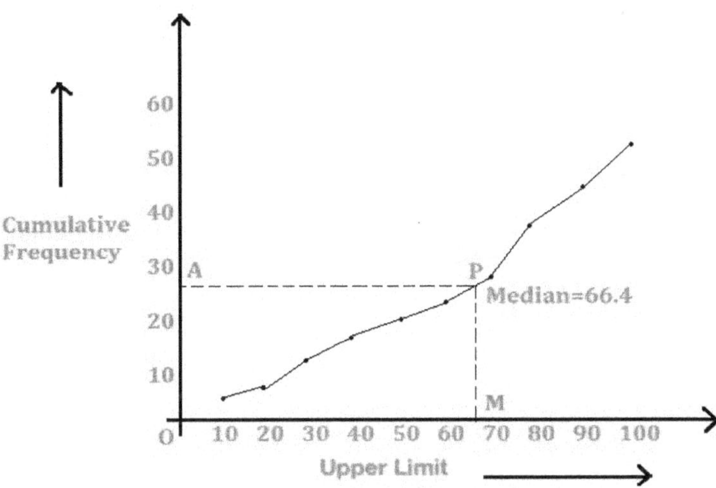

Fig 2.1 Less than cumulative frequency curve

2.3.6.6 More than cumulative frequency

Interval	Frequency
5-10	20
10-15	4
15-20	5

In the above table, we have intervals and frequencies now we are going to find more than the cumulative frequency:

Interval	Frequency	cumulative frequency	Lower Limit
5-10	20	20	5
10-15	4	20-4=16	10
15-20	5	16-5=11	15

How to draw more than cumulative frequency curve: In this instance, the curve is drawn using the classes' lower limit. Here is how to plot a more than Cumulative Frequency curve step-by-step:

1. Mark the matching cumulative frequencies along the y-axis and the lower class limits along the x-axis on a graph paper.
2. By joining these locations one after the other using line segments, we can create a polygon called a cumulative frequency polygon.
3. A curve known as a cumulative frequency graph is created by joining these spots one after the other with a smooth curve.
4. We consider P to be where the less than and more than curves connect. Cut the x-axis at M and draw PM $\perp$ to the y-axis.
5. Then, median equals OM length.

Question: For the given frequency distribution, draw a cumulative frequency graph of more than type and find the median value.

Class interval	0-10	10-20	20-30	30-40	40-50	50-60	60-70
Frequency	5	15	20	20	17	11	9

Solution: For the given table, we have to prepare the more than series as shown below

More than 60	9
More than 50	20
More than 40	37
More than 30	60
More than 20	80
More than 10	95
More than 5	100

Scale: Along the x-axis, 10 small div. = 5.

Along the y-axis, 1 small div.= 1.

Plot all the points A(5, 100), B(10, 95), C(20, 80), D(30, 60), E(40, 37), F(50, 20) and G(60, 9).

Join AB, BC, CD, DE, EF and FG with a freehand, and we will get the required curve, as shown in below figure.

Here, N = 100

$\Rightarrow$ N/2 = 50

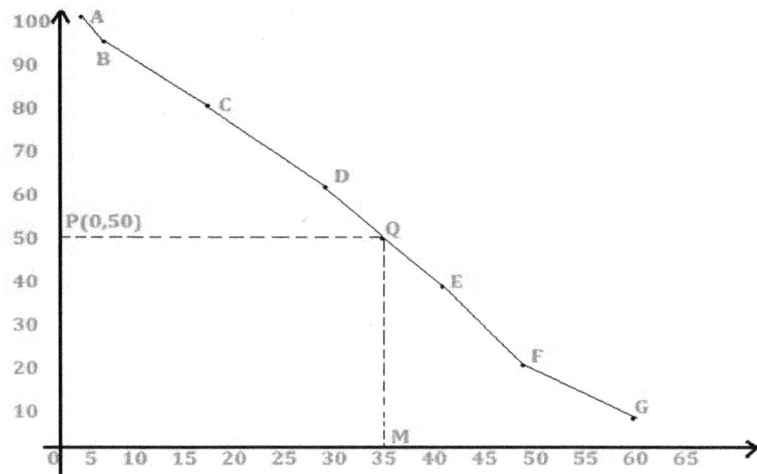

Fig 2.2 More than cumulative frequency curve

From P(0, 50) draw PQ ∥ x-axis, meeting the curve at Q. Draw QM ⊥ OZ, meeting x-axis at M. Clearly, OM = 35 units

Hence, median = 35.

2.3.6.7 Practice Problems on Cumulative frequency Curve

Question 1: Draw a less than cumulative frequency graph for the following data and find the median:

Class Interval	Frequency
10-20	8
20-30	12
30-40	15
40-50	10

Question 2: Create a more than cumulative frequency table and graph for the following data:

Class Interval	Frequency
0-5	7
5-10	13
10-15	15

2.4 Frequency Distribution Graphs: There are several ways to depict the frequency distribution, including pie charts, bar graphs, frequency polygons, and histograms.

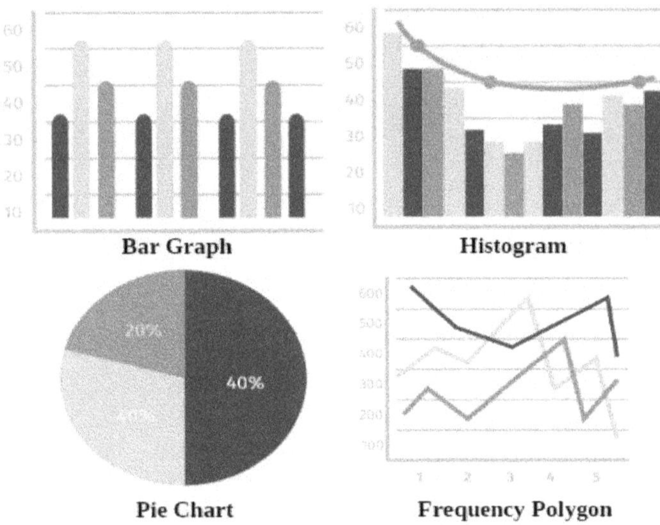

Fig 2.3 Frequency Distribution Graphs

2.4.1 How to graph a frequency distribution

One can graph frequency distributions using pie charts, bar charts, and histograms. The type of variable and the message you want to convey will determine the best option.

Pie chart: A graph that displays a nominal variable's relative frequency distribution is called a pie chart. A circle with one slice for each value is called a pie chart. The slices' relative frequency is shown by their size. When you wish to show the general composition of a variable or highlight a particular variable's frequency or infrequency, this kind of graph can be a useful option.

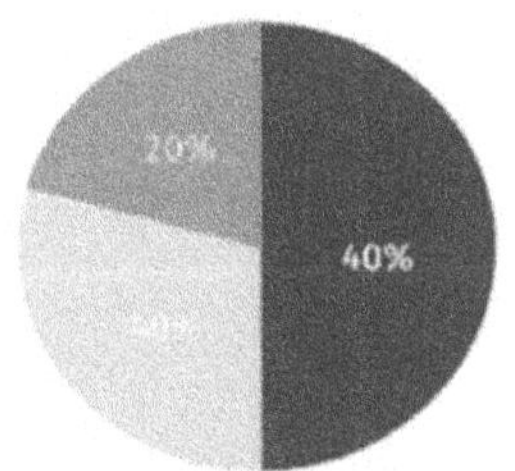

Fig 2.4 Pie Chart

Bar chart: A bar chart is a graph that displays a categorical variable's frequency or relative frequency distribution (nominal or ordinal) (Sundaram KR et al. 2010). The bars' x-axis displays the values, while the y-axis displays the frequencies or relative frequencies. A bar is used to symbolize each value, and the bar's height or length indicates how frequently the value occurs.

When comparing the frequency of various values, a bar chart is a useful tool. Bar heights are considerably simpler to compare than pie chart slice angles.

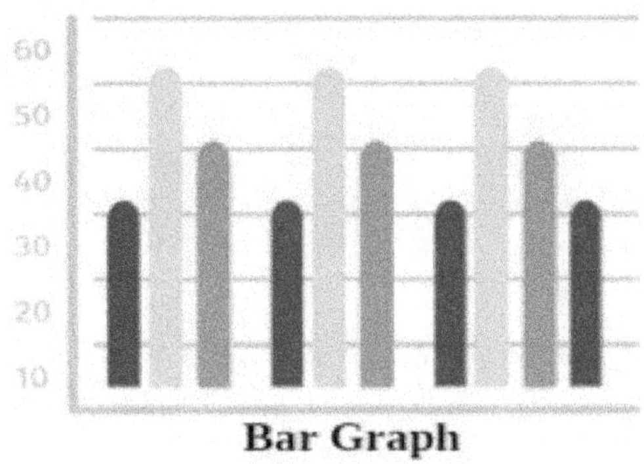

Fig 2.5 Bar Graph

Histogram: A graph that displays a quantitative variable's frequency or relative frequency distribution is called a histogram. It has a bar chart-like appearance. Like a grouped frequency table, the continuous variable is divided into interval groups. The bars' x-axis displays the interval classes, while the y-axis displays the frequencies or relative frequencies. A bar is used to symbolize each interval class, and the bar's height indicates the interval class's frequency or relative frequency.

A histogram is a useful visual representation of a variable's key attributes. A variable's central tendency, variability, and the probability distribution it seems to follow—such as a normal, Poisson, or uniform distribution—can all be seen at a glance.

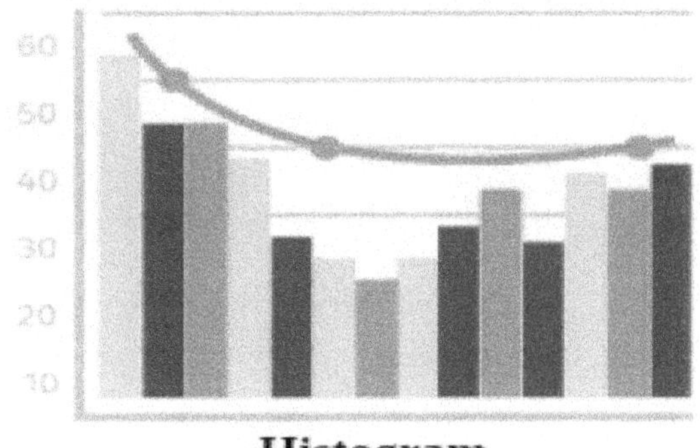

Fig 2.6 Histogram

2.5 Frequency Distribution Curve

The frequency distribution of a data collection is represented graphically by a frequency distribution curve, sometimes referred to as a frequency curve. It is employed to display the frequency and distribution of values or observations in a dataset. Let's examine its various forms according to their shapes as follows:

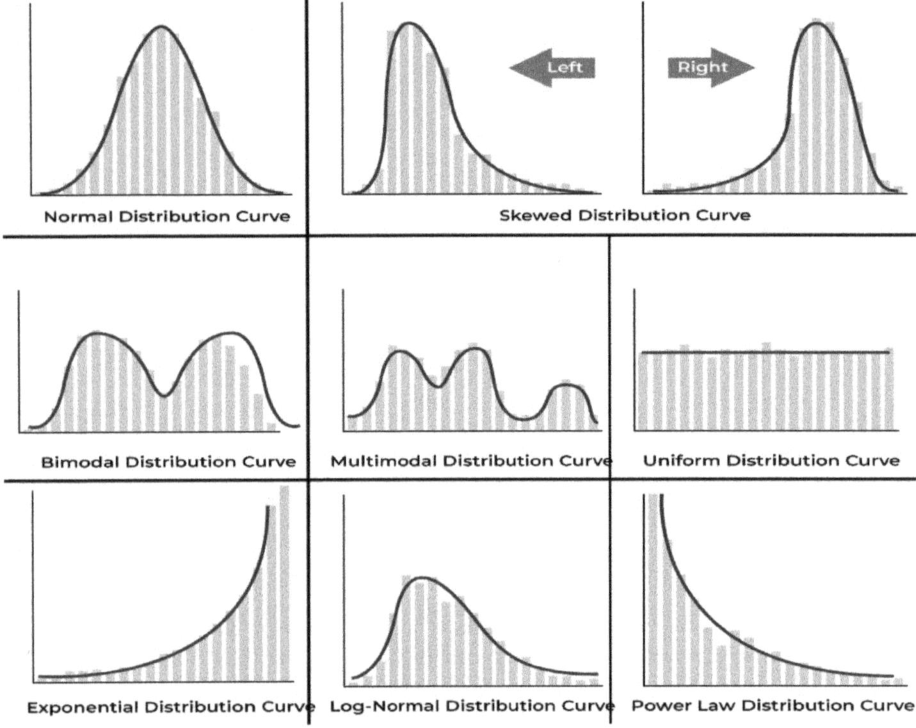

Fig 2.7 Frequency Distribution Curve

2.6 Conclusion – Frequency Distribution

An important statistical tool that offers a succinct overview of the prevalence of each value or category within a dataset is the frequency distribution. It provides a numerical and visual depiction of the dataset's structure by grouping data and displaying the relevant frequencies. With a greater comprehension of the value distribution made possible by this method, we can more successfully spot patterns, trends, and anomalies. We may evaluate important features including central tendency, variability, and the general form of the data distribution using frequency distribution. It makes complicated datasets easier to understand and analyze by simplifying them. This in turn makes it easier to make well-informed decisions, increases the precision of inferences made from the data, and improves the dissemination of findings to interested parties.

As a basis for thorough data analysis and statistical interpretation, frequency distribution is a potent analytical technique that connects unprocessed data with useful insights. It is an essential instrument for comprehending and utilizing the potential of data in a variety of disciplines due to its simplicity and adaptability.

Chapter 3: CHARACTERISTICS OF FREQUENCY DISTRIBUTION

There are four characteristics of Frequency Distribution

- ➢ Measures of central tendency and location (mean, median, mode)
- ➢ Measures of dispersion (range, variance, standard deviation)
- ➢ The extent of symmetry/asymmetry (skewness)
- ➢ The flatness or peaked ness (kurtosis).

3.1 Measures of central tendency and location in statistics

In statistics, central tendencies are the numerical values that are used to reflect the central or mid-value of a sizable set of numerical data. In the field of statistics, these numerical values are referred to as central or average values. Any statistical data or series' central or average value is the variables value that best captures the whole set of data or the frequency distribution that goes along with it. This value is very important since it shows the nature or features of the whole data, which is otherwise very hard to see (Freund, J.E et al., 2006).

According to Bordens and Abbott (2011), measures of central tendency yield a single value that represents the overall size of the data and, by locating the value at or close to the data's central position, offers information about the data's properties. Measures of central tendency are summarized figures that aid in characterizing a central position for a particular set of scores, according to King and Minium (2013).

Measures of central tendency are "a sort of average or typical value of the items in the series and its function is to summarise the series in terms of this average value," according to (Tate 1955).

Measures of central tendency serve the following primary purposes: They offer a summary figure that clearly illustrates the primary placement of all the data. We can gain a sense of the entire data by calculating the average of a particular group.

- ➢ It is simple to condense a large amount of data into a single figure. For big data sets, the mean, median, and mode can be calculated, and a single figure can be produced.
- ➢ Calculating the mean for a particular sample will assist in determining the population mean.
- ➢ Certain decisions will be aided by the outcomes of the computation of measures of central tendency. This is true not only for research judgments but also for decisions that may be applied in a variety of fields, such as policymaking, marketing, sales, and so forth.
- ➢ Measures of central tendency can be used to compute single figures on which comparisons can be made. For instance, it is possible to examine the mean scores earned by boys and girls in relation to the performance of the students on the mathematics examination.

3.1.1 Why Are Central Tendency Metrics Important?

Simplicity: They are simple in that they provide a brief overview of your data set. When someone inquires for the average score on an exam, for example, providing the mean is a smart approach.

Comparison: The process of comparing two or more data sets is simple. August was generally warmer, as you can see if the mean temperature in July was 78°F and in August it was 85°F.

Bases for Other Analyses: The mean or other central measures must be used in the calculations of many statistical tests and models (Moore et al., 2018).

3.1.2 A good central tendency measure should have the following attributes (Bland M et al., 2003):

I.   A precise and well-defined characterization of the core tendency is required. It must not be influenced by personal prejudice and should not be open to several interpretations. Rigidity in the definition is necessary to produce a stable value that accurately depicts the data.

II.   The central tendency measure need to be simple to compute and comprehend. There shouldn't be any complex mathematical computations involved.

III.   The entire set of data must be calculated in order for the value derived from the computation of measures of central tendency to be representative of the data.

IV.   The data needs to be collected from a sample that truly represents the population. The sample thus needs to be randomly selected.

V.   The measure of central tendency needs to display sampling stability and should not be affected by any fluctuations in the sample. For example, if two different researchers obtain a representative sample from a same population, the means computed by them for their respective sample should display least variation.

VI.   The measure of central tendency should not be affected by outliers. Outliers are extreme values in data or distribution.

VII.   The measure of central tendency should render itself to further mathematical computations.

3.2 Different types of measures of Central Tendency

Since the idea of central tendency is now well understood, we will move on to talk about its five metrics. We shall be talking about five measures of central tendency, which are

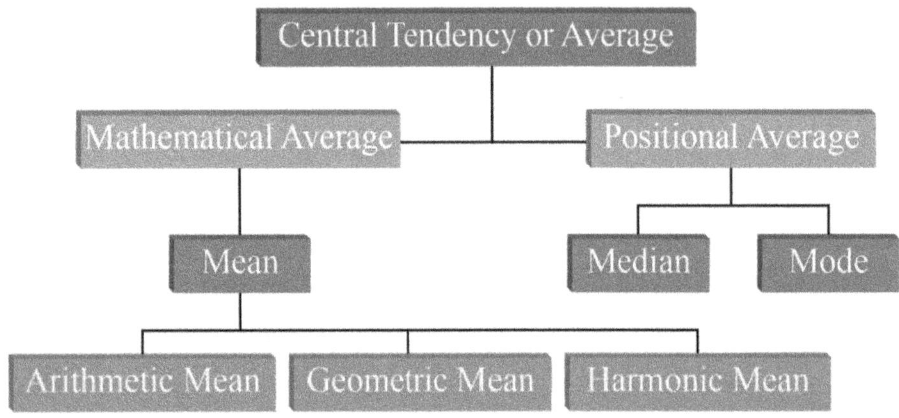

Fig 3.1 Different types of measures of Central Tendency

1) Mean or Arithmetic mean

2) Median

3) Mode

4) Geometric Mean

5) Harmonic Mean

3.3 Mean or Arithmetic mean: The sample mean is represented by the notation "M or $\bar{x}$ ('x-bar')". where "μ" (mu) represents the population mean. Often called average, it is one of the most often used metrics for assessing central tendency. Given that all of the data's scores are taken into account during computation, it can also be referred to as one of the most sensitive measures of central tendency (Bordens and Abbott, 2011). The mean can be used to calculate additional statistical approaches, which increases its usefulness.

The mean is calculated by dividing the total number of scores in the data by the sum of all the scores. For instance, to determine the mean or average score that a class of 100 students received on a psychology examination, we would sum up all of their scores and divide that total by 100, the number of students.

3.3.1 Central tendency measurements computation in grouped and ungrouped data

Now that we have a understanding of the Mean one of the types of measures of central tendency, we will learn how to calculate Mean for both grouped and ungrouped data.

Ungrouped data: Ungrouped data is any information that has not been assigned a classification. We have three people, for instance: one who is twenty-five, another who is thirty, and a third who is fifty. These are ungrouped data since they are individual figures that aren't arranged in any way.

Grouped data: Data that has been categorized or organized is referred to as grouped data. Frequency distribution is the primary method used to organize such data. For instance, we can have age ranges of 26–30, 31–35, 36–40, and so forth. Grouped data is useful, particularly for huge data sets.

How to Calculate Mean

- The population mean of m numbers $x_1, x_2, ..., x_m$ (the data for every member of a population of size m) is denoted by μ and is computed as follows (Hozo SP et al.,2005):

$$\mu = \frac{x_1 + x_2 + \cdots + x_m}{m}$$

- The sample mean of the numbers $x_1, x_2, ..., x_n$ (data for a sample of size n from the population) is denoted by $\bar{x}$ and is computed similarly:

$$\bar{x} = \frac{x_1 + x_2 + \cdots + x_n}{n}$$

3.3.2 Computation of Mean for Individual Series/Ungrouped Data

The formula for computing mean for ungrouped data is

$M = \Sigma X / N$

Where,

M = Mean

ΣX = Summation of scores in the distribution

N = Total number of scores

Example: Consider the following set of data, showing the number of times a sample of 5 students check their e-mail per day: 1, 3, 5, 5, 3.

Here n = 5 and

x1 = 1, x2 = 3, x3 = 5, x4 = 5 and x5 = 3.

Calculate the sample mean

$$\bar{x} = \frac{x_1 + x_2 + \cdots + x_n}{n} = \frac{\Sigma X_i}{n} = 3.4$$

The scores obtained by 10 students on psychology test are as follows:
58 34 32 47 74 67 35 34 30 39
Sol. In order to obtain mean for the above data we will first add the marks
to obtain ΣX:
58+ 34+ 32+ 47+ 74+ 67+ 35+ 34+ 30+ 39 = 450
Now using the formula, we will compute mean
$M = \Sigma X / N$
ΣX = 450 , N= 10 (Total number of students)
Thus,
M= 450/ 10 = 45
Thus, the mean obtained for the above data is 45

3.3.3 Computation of Mean for Grouped Data

The formula for computing mean for grouped data is

$M = \Sigma fX / N$

Where,

M= Mean

Σ= Summation

X= Midpoint of the distribution

f = The respective frequency

N = Total number of scores.

Example: A class of 30 students were given a psychology test and the marks obtained bythem were categorised in to six categories. The lowest marks obtained were 10 and highest mark obtained were 35. A class interval of 5 was employed. The data is given as follows:

Table for the calculation of Mean

Marks	Frequency(f)	MidPoints(x)	fx
10-20	8	15	120
20-30	6	25	150
30-40	7	35	245
40-50	2	45	90
50-60	8	55	440
60-70	2	65	130
	N=33		ΣfX =1175

Solution: Mean = $\dfrac{\Sigma fX}{N} = \dfrac{1175}{33} = 35.60$

Thus, the mean obtained is 35.60

Example: A class of 16 boys has an average weight of 50.25 kg, while the remaining 8 boys have an average weight of 45.15 kg. Calculate the average weight of all boys in the class.

Sol. 16 boys in a class have an average weight of 50.25kg

8 boys in a class have an average weight of 45.15kg

Thus, the required average = [(50.25×16) + (45.15×8)] / (16 + 8)

= (804+361.20) / 24

∴ Required average = 1165.20 / 24

= 48.55 kg

Therefore, the average weight of all boys in the class is 48.55 kg.

3.3.4 Computation of Mean by Shortcut Method (with Assumed mean)

With a small adjustment, the calculations can be made simpler utilizing the previously mentioned assumed mean technique, much like in the case of individual series. Since each item's frequency (f) is provided here, we obtain fd by multiplying each deviation (d) by the frequency.

Next, we obtain Σ fd. Getting the sum of all frequencies, or Σ f, is the next step. Next, determine "Σ fd" / "Σ f." Lastly, the arithmetic mean is determined using

$$\bar{X} = A + \frac{\Sigma\, fd}{\Sigma\, f}$$

Where,

AM= Assumed mean,

Σ = Summation

i = Class interval

$d = \{(X - AM)\}$, X the midpoint of the scores in the interval

f = the respective frequency of the midpoint

N = The total number of frequencies or students.

Let us discuss the steps followed for computation of mean with the help of an example given below:

C-I	10-25	25-40	40-55	55-70	70-85	85-100
Frequency	2	3	7	6	6	6

Solution

Table for the calculation of Mean

CI	Frequency(f_i)	X_i	$d_i = X_i - A$	$f_i d_i$
10-25	2	17.5	-30	-60
25-40	3	32.5	-15	-45
40-55	7	47.5=a	0	0

55-70	6	62.5	15	90
70-85	6	77.5	30	180
85-100	6	92.5	45	270
	$\Sigma f_i = 30$			$\Sigma f_i d_i = 435$

$$\bar{X} = A + \frac{\Sigma f_i d_i}{\Sigma f} = 47.5 + \frac{435}{30} = 60$$

Thus, mean is obtained as 60

And if you refer to the mean obtained by the direct method and mean obtained with the shortcut method, the mean is the same, that is 60

3.3.5 Computation of Mean by using Step Deviation Method

In this case, the deviations are divided by the common factor 'c' which simplifies the calculation. Here we estimate $d' = \frac{d}{c} = \frac{X-A}{c}$

In order to reduce the size of numerical figures for easier calculation. Then get fd' and $\Sigma fd'$.

The formula for arithmetic mean using step deviation method is given as,

$$\bar{X} = A + \frac{\Sigma fd'}{\Sigma f} \times c$$

The following is the cumulative frequency distribution (of less than type) of 1000 persons, each one of age 20 years and above. Determine the mean age.

C-I	20-30	30-40	40-50	50-60	60-70	70-80
Frequency	100	120	130	400	200	50

Solution:

Table for the calculation of Mean

C-1	Frequency	X_i	$d' = \frac{X_i - A}{c}$	$f_i d'_i$

20-30	100	25	-3	-300
30-40	120	35	-2	-240
40-50	130	45	-1	-130
50-60	400	55=a	0	0
60-70	200	65	1	200
70-80	50	75	2	100
	Σf_i=1000			$\Sigma f_i d'_i$=-370

$$\overline{X} = A + \frac{\Sigma fd'}{\Sigma f} \times c$$

$$=55 + \frac{-370}{1000} \times 10$$

$$=55-3.7$$

$$=51.3$$

Thus, mean is obtained as 51.3

3.3.6 Merits of Mean

- ➢ It is simple to compute and understand. It is the most popular central tendency measure because of this.
- ➢ Since each component is a part of the calculation, it has an effect. Because the mathematical formula is inflexible, the outcome stays the same. For this measure of central tendency, fluctuations are negligible when multiple samples are taken from the same population.
- ➢ It can be treated algebraically, in contrast to other measures like the mode and median. One advantage of A.M. is that it is a calculated number independent of the words in a series.
- ➢ It is mostly used to compare concerns because of its stringent definition.

3.3.7 Demerits of Mean

- ➢ It is not graphically located.
- ➢ It will only be helpful if the frequency is dispersed consistently. The results will be ineffective if the skewness is higher.
- ➢ Extreme values or outliers may affect the mean.

- The mean cannot be calculated when there are open-ended classes, such as those with scores of 10 or higher or lower than 5. In these situations, the median and mode can be calculated. This is primarily due to the fact that it is impossible to calculate the midpoint of such distributions.
- The mean cannot be calculated if a score in the data is absent, lost, or unclear unless the mean is calculated for the remaining data without taking the lost score into account and discarding it entirely.
- Inspection cannot be used to establish the mean. Furthermore, a graph cannot be used to determine it.
- It is not appropriate for very asymmetrical or skewed data because the mean will not accurately reflect the data in these situations.

3.3.8 Properties of Mean

- The mean, or average, of a distribution will fluctuate if a new score is added because the mean is sensitive to the precise placement of each and every score within the distribution. For instance, the average of the scores are 5, 4, 6, 3, and 2. [We calculated the total number of scores (N) by adding 5+4+6+3+2=20 and dividing the result by 5 to get the value 4]. However, the mean will be 4.67 if the scores are changed to 5, 4, 6, 3, 2, 8. [By adding 5+4+6+3+2+8=28 and dividing it by 6, which is the total number of scores (N), we obtained the result 4.67.]

- According to King and Minium (2013), the mean represents the equilibrium point of any distribution, and the sum of the positive and negative deviations from the mean is equal.

- The mean works particularly well when we want the central tendency measure to represent the total of the scores.

3.4 Median: A distribution's median is the point below and above which half of the scores fall. P50 is another name for the median (King and Minium, 2008). "Md" is the sign for median. Bordens and Abbott (2011, page 411) state that "In an ordered distribution, the median is the middle score. The variable that splits the distribution into two equal parts—one with all values larger than or equal to the median value, and the other with all values less than or equal to it—is called the median. When the data set is sorted by magnitude, the "middle" element is the median. Since the position of various values determines the median, it is unaffected, for example, by an increase in the magnitude of the greatest value (Manikandan S et al., 2011). The median in this distribution is then determined to be the middle score. While this can appear simple for an odd number of scores (Altman DG et al., 1991), when there are an even number of scores are calculated using a specific process that will be covered when we study how to calculate the median later in this section.

3.4.1 Computation of Median for Ungrouped Data

For ungrouped data two situations are their in the calculation of the median.

a) When N is odd

b) When N is even.

Where N is odd median can be calculated by formula

Median= $\dfrac{(N+1)^{th}}{2}$

When the N is even numbers of scores, When N is even the medians can be calculated by following formula. The value of (N/2) the item the value of (N/2) + 1 the item

Median= $\dfrac{\left[\frac{N}{2}\right]^{th} item + \left[\frac{N}{2}+1\right]^{th} item}{2}$

Odd Data: Suppose we have the following scores, 17,14,15,25,44,32,30. Find the Median?
Solution: First we will arrange the above scores in ascending order : 14,15,17,25,44,32,30
Here N=7 ,

M= (N+1)/2 = 4
the 4th item
i.e. 25 is the median.
The scored 25 has lies in the middle of the series three scores lies above and three score lies below 25.

Even data: When the data is even, the median is computed in the

Following manner: 58 34 32 47 74 67 35 34 30 39 (N= 10)

First the data is to be arranged in either ascending or descending order.

We will arrange the data in ascending order and it will look like this:

30 32 34 34 35 39 47 58 67 74

The following formula is used to compute median:

Md = (N/2)th score + [(N/2)th score + 1]/ 2

The (N/2)th score is the 5th score, that is 35.

The (N/2)th score + 1 is the 6th score, that is 39.

Thus, Md =35 +39/ 2= 37

The median thus obtained is 37.

3.4.2 Computation of Median in case of discrete series

In case of discrete series the position of median and odd no of observation i.e.

Median= $\frac{(N+1)}{2}$ item, can be located through cumulative frequency. The corresponding value at this position is the value of median.

The median formula of a given set of numbers say having 'n' even numbers of observations, can be expressed as:

$$\text{Median}= \frac{\left[\frac{N}{2}\right]^{th} item+\left[\frac{N}{2}+1\right]^{th} item}{2}$$

Example 1: Find median of the following discrete Frequency distribution

Items	5	7	9	12	16	20
Frequency	1	6	4	5	7	2

Solution:

Table for the calculation of Median

Items	Freq	Cumulative frequency(cf)
5	1	1
7	6	1+6=7
9	4	7+4=11
12	5	11+5=16
16	7	16+7=23
20	2	23+2=24
	$\sum f_i = 24$	

$$\text{Median}= \frac{\left[\frac{N}{2}\right]^{th} item+\left[\frac{24}{2}+1\right]^{th} item}{2}$$

$$= \frac{\left[\frac{24}{2}\right]^{th} item+\left[\frac{24}{2}+1\right]^{th} item}{2}$$

$$= \frac{[12]^{th}\,item + [13]^{th}\,item}{2}$$

$$= \frac{12+13}{2} = \frac{25}{2} = 12.5$$

Median= 12.5

Example 2: Find median of the following discrete Frequency distribution

Items	50	55	60	65	70	75
Frequency	12	15	20	2	6	9

Solution:

Table for the calculation of Median

X	Frequency	CF
50	12	12
55	15	27
60	20	47
65	2	49
70	6	55
75	9	64
	$\sum f_i = 64$	

$$\text{Median} = \frac{\left[\frac{N}{2}\right]^{th} item + \left[\frac{N}{2}+1\right]^{th} item}{2}$$

$$= \frac{\left[\frac{64}{2}\right]^{th} item + \left[\frac{64}{2}+1\right]^{th} item}{2}$$

$$= \frac{32 + (32+1)}{2}$$

=32.5

Median = 60

3.4.3 Computation of Median in case of Continuous series

In case of continuous frequency distribution the class corresponding to frequency just greater then $\frac{n}{2}$ is called as Median Class.

The value of median is obtained by the following formula

$$Md= l + \frac{\left(\frac{N}{2}-cf\right)}{f} \times h$$

Where,

l = The lower limit of the median class

N = Total of all the frequencies

cf = Sum of frequencies before the median class

f = frequency within the interval upon which the median falls

i = class interval.

Let us discuss the steps followed for computation of median with the help of the example given below:

Q.no: find out median by the following data?

CI	0-10	10-20	20-30	30-40	40-50	50-60	60-70
Frequency	4	13	27	87	51	47	14

Solution.

Table for the calculation of Median

C-I	Freq	CF
0-10	4	4
10-20	13	17
20-30	27	44

30-40	87	131
40-50	51	182
50-60	47	229
60-70	14	243

$$\left(\frac{N}{2}\right)^{th} size = \frac{243}{3} = 121.5$$

$$Median = l + \frac{\left(\frac{N}{2} - cf\right)}{f} \times h$$

$$Median = 30 + \frac{\left(\frac{243}{2} - 44\right)}{87} \times 1030 + 8.90 = 38.90$$

3.4.4 Merits of Median

- ➢ It is simple to grasp and straightforward to compute.
- ➢ The median may frequently be found just by looking at it. Since it is a positional average and independent of magnitude, it is unaffected by the extreme values, that is, the largest and smallest values. Its tight definition gives it a clear and certain worth.
- ➢

  When dealing with qualitative data, when ranking is favored over measuring or counting, the median is the best way to quantify central tendency.
- ➢

  Even if the values of the extremes are unknown, it can still be computed. However, it should be understood how many objects there are.

3.4.5 Demerits of Median

- ➢ When there are many observations, it takes a lot of time to arrange the data in either ascending or descending order of magnitude because the median is an average position.
- ➢ It is a positional average that ignores the components' magnitude. The extreme values are ignored.
- ➢ It cannot be regarded as their good representative because it is not reliant on every observation.
- ➢ It will not be able to represent the data if there is a significant fluctuation in the data.

3.4.6 Properties of the Median

- ➢ The median is less susceptible to outliers or extreme scores than the mean.
- ➢ The median can be employed effectively when a distribution is asymmetrical or skewed.
- ➢ The median can be calculated when a distribution is open-ended, meaning that the exact score at one end of the distribution is unknown.

3.5 Mode: The value that frequently occurs in the data set is the mode, which is a measure of central tendency. The mode is represented as the highest bar on a bar chart or histogram. There is a mode in the data set if there are some values that appear repeatedly. There is no mode in the data if there are no repeated values. The mode is typically applied to discrete, category, and ordinal data (Manikandan S et al., 2011). Furthermore, the mode is the only metric that makes use of category data. Take the most popular flavored ice cream, for example. It is the value that appears most frequently in the set of observations and that either item in the set clusters closely around. "Mo" is the sign for mode. The score that appears most frequently in a distribution is called the mode. Using the previously discussed psychology test scores of a group of 100 students, if out of these 100. Ten of the pupils received 35 points. Therefore, 35 is the value that appears the most frequently and will be referred to as the mode. Additionally, some distributions may have two modes, or be bimodal. For example, if 10 more students in this 100-student group received 47 marks, 47 is the value that occurs as frequently as 35 and will therefore be referred to as the mode in addition to 35. Similarly, the terms trimodal and trimodal are used when there are three modes.

However, there might not be a mode in a distribution if the scores differ significantly. Because it only considers the most common scores, the mode by itself does not adequately characterize the distribution. Any other scores are not taken into account (Norman GR et al., 2000).

3.5.1 Computation of Mode for Ungrouped Data

Now, let's see how to calculate the mode of ungrouped data using the example that follows:
35 34 30 39 74 67 58 34 32 47

The simplest way to determine the mode is to simply count the scores that occur the most times in the data. In our example, the score appears twice, with a maximum frequency of 34. 34 is the mode as a result.

3.5.2 Computation of Mode for Discrete frequency distribution

Mode is the value of variable which is prominent in the series. Thus in case of discrete frequency distribution.

For example find Mode?

X	1	2	3	4	5	6	7	8
Frequency	4	9	16	25	22	15	7	3

The value of X corresponding to Maximum frequency based 25 is 4

Mode =4, mode is value of X corresponding to maximum frequency

3.5.3 Computation of Mode for Continuous frequency distribution

In case of Continuous frequency Distribution the formula of Mode is

$$\text{Mode} = l + \frac{(f_1 - f_0)}{2f_1 - f_0 - f_2} \times h$$

Where,

l = Lower limit of modal class

$f1$ = Frequency of modal class

$f0$ = Frequency of class preceding the modal class

$f2$ = Frequency of the class succeeding the modal class

i = Class interval of the modal class

Let us discuss the steps followed for computation of mode with the help of the

example given below:

Example: Find out Mode for the following data?

Marks of Student	0-10	10-20	20-30	30-40	40-50	50-60	60-70
Frequency	6	5	8	15	7	6	3

Solution

Table for the calculation of Mode

C-I	Frequency
0-10	6
10-20	5
20-30	8
30-40	15
40-50	7
50-60	6
60-70	3

$$\text{Mode} = l + \frac{(f_1 - f_0)}{2f_1 - f_0 - f_2} \times h$$

$$= 30 + \frac{(15 - 8)}{2 \times 15 - 8 - 7} \times 10$$

$$= 30 - \frac{(7)}{15} \times 10 = 30 - 4.666 = 34.6666$$

3.5.4 Properties of Mode

1) Mode can be used with variables that can be measured on nominal scale.
2) Mode is easier to compute than mean and media. But it is not used often because of lack of stability from one sample to another and also because a single set of data may possibly have more than one mode. Also, when there is more than one mode, then the modes cannot be termed to adequately measure central location.
3) Mode is not affected by outliers or extreme scores.

3.5.5 Merits of Mode

➢ It is very easy to calculate. In some cases it can be determined just by observation or inspection.

➢ Everyone understands the concept of majority. Since, mode is based on this concept, it is easy to understand.
➢ It is a value around which there is maximum concentration of observations. Hence, it is the best representative of the data.
➢ It can be determined graphically with the help of Histogram.

3.5.6 Demerits of Mode
➢ Since the mode takes into account only the highest concentration of frequencies, its value is not dependent on every item in the series.
➢ It's not always possible to ascertain the value of the mode.
➢ Bi-, tri-, or multi-modal distributions are possible.
➢ Sampling irregularities have a significant impact on mode.
➢ In the case of Mean, this effect is greater.

3.6 Geometric Mean (GM)

In statistics and mathematics, measurements of central tendency make it simple to explain the summary that characterizes the values of the entire data set. The mean, median, mode, and range are the most crucial indicators of central tendencies. Out of them, the data set mean will give the general sense of the data. The average of numbers is defined by the mean. There are three distinct kinds of means: harmonic mean (HM), geometric mean (GM), and arithmetic mean (AM) (Dawson B et al., 2004).

3.6.1 Definition of Geometric Mean (GM)
A geometric mean is a mean or average that uses the product of a set of values to display the central tendency of the data. A geometric mean is the nth root of the product of a collection of n observations. For a set of numbers $x_1, x_2, \ldots, x_n$, the geometric mean, or G.M., is provided as

$$G.M. = (x_1 . x_2 . \ldots . x_n)^{\frac{1}{n}}$$

Or, $G.M. = \sqrt[n]{x_1 . x_2 . \ldots . x_n}$

The nth root of the product of n numbers is the definition of the geometric mean, for example. The geometric mean differs from the arithmetic mean, as can be observed. Because the data values are added and then divided by the total number of values in an arithmetic mean. In geometric mean, on the other hand, we multiply the indicated data values and then use the radical index to find the root for the total number of data values. For instance, taking the square root of two data, the cube root of three data, the fourth root of four data values, and so on are examples.

For example: for a given set of two numbers such as 3 and 1, the geometric mean is equal to $\sqrt{(3 \times 1)} = \sqrt{3} = 1.732$.

3.6.2 Computation of Geometric Mean in case of ungrouped data

The geometric mean is the square root of the product of the two items in the data series, if there are any. The geometric mean of three items is equal to the cube root of the product of three items. The geometric mean of a series of 'n' items is equal to the nth root of the product of those things. Let's put it in symbolic form:

$$\text{Geometric Mean} = \sqrt[n]{X_1 . X_2 . \, \dots . \, X_n}$$

where $X_1, X_2, \dots, X_n$ refer to the 'n' items of the series

For example, we have three numbers 4, 8, and 16, the geometric mean of these three numbers would be:

$$\text{Geometric Mean} = \sqrt[3]{X_1 . X_2 \, \dots .. \, X_3} = \sqrt[3]{512} = 8$$

The average derived from the product of objects is hence known as the geometric mean. It gets challenging to locate their goods and identify its origins when there are three or more products. Thus, the logarithm can be used to simplify calculations.

> The steps are as follows:
> ➢ Calculate the logarithm of the variable's various values, then add them up; log x.
> ➢ After dividing it by 'n' (the number of pieces), find the value's antilogarithm. The Geometric Mean is thus obtained.

Symbolically it can be expressed as follows:

$$\text{Log GM} = nlog(X_1 . X_2 \dots \dots . X_n)$$

$$= \frac{\log(X_1 + X_2 + \dots \dots + X_n)}{n}$$

$$= \frac{\Sigma logX}{n}$$

Therefore $\text{GM} = \text{Antilog} \, \dfrac{(\Sigma logX)}{n}$

For example, geometric mean of four numbers 20, 65, 83 and 135 will be

$$\text{GM} = \text{Antilog} \, \frac{(\Sigma logX)}{n}$$

$$= \text{Antilog} \frac{(log20 + log60 + log83 + log135}{4}$$

$$= \text{Antilog } (1.7908) = 61.77$$

Question: Find the G.M of the values 10, 25, 5, and 30

Solution: Given 10, 25, 5, 30

We know that,

$$GM = \sqrt[n]{X_1 . X_2 \dots . X_n}$$

$$= \sqrt[4]{10.25.5.30}$$

$$= \sqrt[4]{37500}$$

$$= 13.915$$

Therefore, the geometric mean = 13.915

Question: Find the geometric mean of the following data.

45, 60, 48, 100, 65.

Sol.

Table for the calculation of Geometric Mean

Weight of ear x(g)	logx
45	1.653
60	1.778
48	1.681
100	2.000
65	1.813
total	8.925

$$GM = Antilog \frac{(\sum \log X)}{n}$$

$$= Antilog \frac{(8.925)}{5}$$

$$= Antilog(1.785)$$

$$= 60.95$$

Therefore the G.M of the given data is 60.95

3.6.3 Computation of Geometric Mean in case of Grouped data

We should now talk about the process for grouping data. As you are aware, the grouped data may be in the form of continuous or discrete series, and we must adhere to distinct protocols for each type of series.

Discrete Series: The geometric mean is calculated as follows when the data is grouped, that is, when it takes the shape of a frequency distribution:

Discrete Series: When the data is grouped data i.e., in the form of a frequency distribution, the geometric mean is computed as follows:

$$GM = \sqrt[n]{X_1^{f_1}.X_2^{f_2} \ ..... X_r^{f_r}}$$

where $X_1, X_2 \ ....X_r$ are the different values of the variate x with their respective frequencies $f_1, f_2 \ ....f_r$ and n= $f_1 + f_2 + \cdots ..... +f_r = \sum f$

$$\text{Log G. M} = \frac{1}{n}(f_1 \log X_1 + f_2 \log X_2 + .. + f_r \log X_r)$$

$$= \frac{1}{n}(\sum f \log X)$$

$$\text{G. M} = Antilog \frac{1}{n}(\sum f \log X)$$

Example: Find the Geometric mean for the following

weight of sorghum (x)	No. of ear head(f)
50	5
63	10

65	5
130	15
135	15

Solution:

Table for the calculation of Geometric Mean

weight of sorghum (x)	No. of ear head(f)	$Logx$	$fLogx$
50	5	1.699	8.495
63	10	1.799	17.99
65	5	1.813	9.065
130	15	2.114	31.71
135	15	2.130	31.95
Total	50	9.555	99.21

$$GM = Antilog\frac{(\sum flogX)}{n} = Antilog\frac{(99.21)}{50}$$

$$= Antilog(1.9842) = 96.43$$

3.6.4 Computation of Geometric Mean in case of Continuous Series: The only change in the earlier formula of geometric mean is that you replace 'x' by 'm' which is the mid-value of classes.

$$G.M = Antilog\frac{1}{n}(\sum flogm)$$

The steps taken in both formulations are as follows:
- Create logarithms from the supplied variate x values or, in the case of continuous series, the mid-value (m).
- The result of multiplying them by the corresponding frequencies is either $\sum flogx$ or $\sum flogm$

➤ Calculate the antilogarithm of the result by dividing the product by the overall frequency $\sum f = n$.

Question: Find the geometric mean of the following grouped data for the frequency distribution of weights.

Weight of ear heads (g)	60-80	80-100	100-120	120-140	140-160
No of ear heads (f)	22	38	45	35	20

Solution:

Table for the calculation of Geometric Mean

Weight of ear heads (x)	No of ear heads (f)	Mid m	Log m	flogm
60-80	22	70	1.845	40.59
80-100	38	90	1.945	74.25
100-120	45	110	2.041	91.85
120-140	35	130	2.114	73.99
140-160	20	150	2.176	43.52
Total	160			324.2

From the given data, n = 160

We know that the G.M for the grouped data is

$$\text{G.M} = \text{Antilog} \frac{1}{n} \left(\sum flogm \right)$$

$$= \text{Antilog}\left(\frac{324.2}{160}\right) = \text{Antilog}(2.02625) = 106.23$$

$$GM = 106.23$$

3.6.5 Merits of Geometric Mean

- ➢ It is predicated on every observation.
- ➢ It has a strict definition.
- ➢ It can receive additional algebraic treatment.
- ➢ Extreme values have less of an impact on it.
- ➢ It can be used to average rates, percentages, and ratios.

3.6.6 Demerits of Geometric Mean

- ➢ It is hard to comprehend.
- ➢ If any of the items in the series are 0 or negative, the geometric mean cannot be calculated.
- ➢ The GM might not be the series' true worth.
- ➢ Instead of highlighting the absolute difference in change, as is the case with the arithmetic mean, it highlights the property of the change ratio.

3.6.7 Properties of Geometric Mean

- ➢ In any given data collection, the arithmetic mean is always greater than the G.M. The product of the objects stays the same if the G.M. is used to replace every object in the data set.
- ➢ The ratio of the geometric means of two series is equal to the ratio of the corresponding observations of the G.M.
- ➢ The product of the geometric mean of two series is the product of the corresponding elements of the G.M.

3.6.8 Application of Geometric Mean

The G.M.'s biggest premise is that data can actually be understood as a scaling factor. We must first choose when to use the G.M. It should only be applied to positive values, according to the answer, and is frequently used for a group of numbers whose values are exponential in nature and intended to be multiplied collectively. As a result, there won't be any zero or negative values that we can actually use. Numerous fields employ the geometric mean because of its many benefits. Here are a few examples of the applications:

- ➢ Stock indices make advantage of it. Because G.M. is employed in many of the value line indexes that finance departments use.

- ➢ It is employed to determine the portfolio's yearly return.
- ➢ It is employed in the field of finance to determine average growth rates, which are also known as compound annual growth rates.
- ➢ Additionally, it is employed in research on bacterial proliferation and cell division, among other topics.

3.7 Harmonic Mean

When determining the average rate or rate of change, the harmonic mean is a type of numerical average that is typically employed. Among the three Pythagorean meanings, it is one. The geometric mean and the arithmetic mean are the other two. Due to their extensive application in the fields of geometry and music, these three means or averages are highly significant. The reciprocal of the average of the reciprocal terms is the definition of the harmonic mean, which can be found in a data series or set of observations. In other words, it is the reciprocal of the reciprocals' arithmetic mean.

3.7.1 What is Harmonic Mean?

The harmonic mean is a measure of central tendency. Say we want to determine a single value that can be used the describe the behaviour of data around a central value. Then such a value is known as a measure of central tendency. In statistics, there are three measures of central tendency. These are the mean, median, and mode. The mean can be further classified into arithmetic mean, geometric mean, and harmonic mean.

3.7.1.1 Harmonic Mean Definition

The harmonic mean is a type of Pythagorean mean. To find it, we divide the number of terms in a data series by the sum of all the reciprocal terms. It will always be the lowest as compared to the geometric and arithmetic mean.

3.7.1.2 Example of Harmonic Mean:

- ➢ Suppose we have a sequence given by 1, 3, 5, 7. The difference between each term is 2. This forms an arithmetic progression.
- ➢ To find the harmonic mean, we take the reciprocal of these terms. This is given as 1, 1/3, 1/5, 1/7 (the sequence forms a harmonic progression).
- ➢ Next, we divide the total number of terms (4) by the sum of the terms (1 + 1/3 + 1/5 + 1/7).
- ➢ Thus, the harmonic mean = 4 / (1 + 1/3 + 1/5 + 1/7) = 2.3864.

3.7.2 Computation of Harmonic Mean

If we have a set of observations given by $x_1, x_2, \ldots, x_n$. The reciprocal terms of this data set will be $\frac{1}{x_1}, \frac{1}{x_2}, \ldots \frac{1}{x_n}$. Thus, the harmonic mean formula is given by

$$\text{HM} = \frac{n}{\left(\dfrac{1}{x_1} + \dfrac{1}{x_2} +, \ldots + \dfrac{1}{x_n}\right)}$$

Here, the total number of observations is divided by the sum of reciprocals of all observations.

$$\text{HM} = \frac{n}{\left(\frac{1}{x_1}+\frac{1}{x_2}+,\ldots+\frac{1}{x_n}\right)}$$

$$= \frac{n}{\sum_{i=1}^{n} \left(\frac{1}{x_i}\right)}$$

H.M is used when we are dealing with speed, rates, etc.

Harmonic Mean Formula

For a Discrete frequency distribution

$$\text{H. M} = \frac{N}{\sum_{i=1}^{n} f_i\left(\frac{1}{x_i}\right)}$$

H.M. for Continuous data:

$$\text{H. M} = \frac{N}{\sum_{i=1}^{n} f_i \left(\frac{1}{x_i}\right)}$$

Where x_i is the mid-point of the class interval

Example: Calculate the harmonic mean for the following data:

X	1	3	5	7	9	11
F	2	4	6	8	10	12

Solution: The calculation for the harmonic mean is shown in the below table:

Table for the calculation of Harmonic Mean

x	F	$\dfrac{1}{x}$	$\dfrac{f}{x}$
1	2	1	2

3	4	0.33	1.33
5	6	0.2	1.2
7	8	0.14	1.14
9	10	0.11	1.11
11	12	0.09	1.09
	N=42		=7.879

$$\text{H. M} = \frac{N}{\sum_{i=1}^{n} f_i \left(\frac{1}{x_i}\right)}$$

$$= \frac{42}{7.879}$$

$$= 5.331$$

Example: The following data is obtained from the survey. Compute H.M ?

X	130	135	140	145	150
f	3	4	8	9	2

Solution:

Table for the calculation of Harmonic Mean

x	f	$\dfrac{f}{x}$
130	3	0.0231
135	4	0.0091

140	8	0.0571
145	9	0.0621
150	2	0.0133
	N=26	0.1648

$$\text{H. M} = \frac{N}{\sum_{i=1}^{n} f_i\left(\frac{1}{x_i}\right)}$$

$$= \frac{26}{0.1648}$$

$$= 157.77$$

Example: Find the harmonic mean of the following distribution of data?

C-I	2-6	6-10	10-14
f	10	12	18

Solution:

Table for the calculation of Harmonic Mean

C-I	Mid point(x)	f	$\frac{f}{x}$
2-6	4	10	2.5
6-10	8	12	1.5
10-14	12	18	1.5
		N=40	=5.5

$$\text{H. M} = \frac{N}{\sum_{i=1}^{n} f_i\left(\frac{1}{x_i}\right)} = \frac{40}{5.5} = 7.27$$

When variables are stated as a ratio of various measuring units, the average of those variables is typically found using this mathematical mean. The benefits and drawbacks of the harmonic mean are listed below:

3.7.3 Merits of the Harmonic Mean

- ➢ It is entirely dependent on observations and is highly effective at averaging specific kinds of rates. Below are some additional benefits of the harmonic mean.
- ➢ It is tightly defined since its value is constant.
- ➢ It is not substantially impacted, even in the event of a sample variation.
- ➢ To find the harmonic mean, every item in the series must be considered.

3.7.4 Demerits of the Harmonic Mean

- ➢ All of the series' components must be known in order to compute this harmonic mean. We are unable to ascertain the harmonic mean when dealing with unknown factors. Other drawbacks of the harmonic mean are listed below.
- ➢ Finding the harmonic mean can be a time-consuming and intricate process.
- ➢ This mean cannot be computed if any of the terms in the provided series are 0.
- ➢ The harmonic mean of a series is significantly impacted by its extreme values.

3.7.5 Properties of Harmonic Mean

Harmonic means possess few properties which make them different from other types of means.

- ➢ The estimated harmonic averages of the data will likewise be c for all the observations at a constant, let's say c.
- ➢ For any series with negative values, the harmonic mean can likewise be calculated.
- ➢ A series' harmonic mean cannot be found if any of its values are zero since there is no reciprocal of zero.
- ➢ The estimated harmonic mean will be lower than the geometric and arithmetic means if all of the values in a given series are neither equal nor zero.
- ➢ The harmonic mean, or AM > GM > HM, has the lowest value when compared to the geometric and arithmetic means.

3.7.6 Uses of Harmonic Mean

The ability to determine multiplicative and divisor relationships between fractions without using a common denominator is a significant characteristic of the harmonic mean. In sectors like finance, this technology can be quite beneficial. Other practical uses of the harmonic mean are listed below.

- ➢ It is useful for figuring out the Fibonacci series' patterns. When evaluating average multiples, it is utilized in the finance industry.
- ➢ Quantities like speed can be calculated with it. This is due to the fact that speed, like km/hr, is stated as a ratio of two measurement units.
- ➢ Because it gives each data point in a sample the same weight, it can also be used to determine the average of rates.

3.7.7 Relation Between AM, GM, and HM

The products of the harmonic mean (HM) and the arithmetic mean (AM) will always be equal to the square of the geometric mean (GM) of the given data set. To understand the relationship between the AM, GM, and GM we will take the help of the formulas. Say we have 2 numbers a and b.

$$n = 2$$

According to definition

$$AM = \frac{(a + b)}{2}$$

$$HM = \frac{2ab}{(a + b)}$$

$$GM = \sqrt{(ab)}$$

Now taking the square we get $GM^2 = (ab)$. Using this value,

$$HM = GM^2 \cdot \left[\frac{2}{a + b)}\right]$$

$$HM = \frac{GM^2}{AM}$$

Thus, we get

$$GM^2 = HM \times AM$$

Also, $HM \leq GM \leq AM$

Note the following:

- ✓ Arithmetic mean is used when the data values have the same units.

- ✓ The geometric mean is used when the data set values have differing units.

- ✓ When the values are expressed in rates we use harmonic mean.

Conclusion

In this chapter, we learned about the various measures of central tendency, which help in identifying a single representative value for a given dataset. We explored the **mean (arithmetic mean)**, which is the sum of all observations divided by the total number of observations and is useful for normally distributed data but sensitive to outliers. We also studied the **median**, which is the middle value in an ordered dataset and is more resistant to extreme values, making it suitable for skewed distributions. The **mode**, which represents the most frequently occurring value, is particularly useful for categorical and discrete data. Additionally, we covered the **geometric mean**, which is calculated as the nth root of the product of n values and is commonly used in financial and growth-related data. Lastly, we examined the **harmonic mean**, which is the reciprocal of the arithmetic mean of reciprocals, making it valuable in rate-based calculations such as speed and efficiency. Each measure has its own significance, and selecting the appropriate one depends on the nature of the dataset and the purpose of analysis. Understanding these measures allows us to summarize data effectively and make informed statistical decisions.

Chapter: 4 Measures of Dispersion or Variability

4.1 Introduction: Measures of Dispersion or Variability

The state of becoming dispersed or spread is called dispersion. The amount of variation that numerical data is likely to exhibit around an average value is known as statistical dispersion. In other words, dispersion aids in comprehending how the data is distributed (Kothari CR 2nd edition).

Measures of dispersion in statistics are useful for interpreting data variability, or determining how homogeneous or heterogeneous the data is. Simply put, it indicates how dispersed or compressed the variable is. Dispersion literally means scatterness. In order to understand homogeneity or heterogeneity of dispersion, we examine dispersion.

4.1.1 Measures of Dispersion Definition

Positive real numbers are known as measures of dispersion, and they indicate how homogenous or heterogeneous the provided data is. A measure of dispersion will have a value of 0 if all of the data points in a data collection are identical. However, the value of the measures of dispersion likewise rises as the data's variability does.

According to L.R Connor: Dispersion is the measure of extent to which individual item is vary.

According to Spiegel: the degree to which numerical data tend to spread about an average value is called the variation or dispersion of data.

Characteristics of an ideal measures of Dispersion

- It should be rigidly defined.
- It should be amenable to further mathematical treatment.

4.1.2 Measures of Dispersion Example

Assume that A = {3, 1, 6, 2} and B = {1, 5, 9, 10} are two data sets. A's population variance is 3.5, while B's population variance is 12.68. This suggests that compared to data set A, data set B is more varied. As a result, the variance facilitates comparing the two data sets, A and B, based on variability.

4.1.3 Significance of Measures of Dispersion

➢ The reliability of an average value is determined by measures of dispersion. To put it another way, measurements of variance highlight the extent to which an average accurately represents the full set of data. When there is less variance, the average depicts the data's individual values relatively accurately, and when variance is high, the average might not accurately reflect all of the units and be highly untrustworthy.

➢ Determining the type and reasons of variations is another goal of measuring them so that the variation itself can be controlled. For instance, variations in product quality within the production process can be examined by the quality control department by determining the cause of the variances in the product's quality. Dispersion measures are therefore useful for managing the sources of variation.

➢ We can compare two or more series based on their variability thanks to the measures of dispersion. The consistency or uniformity may also be determined by the relative measures of dispersion. Reduced relative measure value of dispersion suggests that the data is more consistent or uniform.

4.1.4 Properties of Good Measure of Dispersion

The characteristics of a good average measure and a good dispersion measure are comparable. Therefore, the following characteristics should be present in a good estimate of dispersion:

➢ It must be straightforward to comprehend;
➢ It must be easy to calculate
➢ It must be strictly defined
➢ It must be founded on all data observations
➢ It must be susceptible to additional algebraic treatment
➢ It should not be overly impacted by severe observations, and it should have sampling stability.

4.2 Types of Measures of Dispersion

Two major categories can be used to group the dispersion measures. There are two types of dispersion measurements: absolute and relative. Absolute metrics of deviation include range, variance, standard deviation, and mean deviation (A. M. Goon et al., 2008). The unit of these measurements is the same as that of the data under examination. Relative measurements of deviation are called coefficients of dispersion. Dispersion metrics of this kind are invariably dimensionless. These steps will be covered in more detail in the following sections.

4.3 Absolute Measures of Dispersion

Absolute metrics of dispersion are appropriate when determining the data's dispersion within an experiment. Typically, these metrics convey changes within a dataset in relation to the mean of the observational deviations. The following is a list of the most widely used absolute metrics of deviation.

- Range
- Quartile Deviation
- Mean Deviation
- Standard Deviation and Variance

4.3.1 Range

The most basic way to quantify dispersion is range. It is described as the difference between the variable's maximum and minimum values within the distribution. Its simplicity is what makes it good. Its drawback is that it is a rough metric since it solely uses the variable's maximum and minimum observations (Malhotra NK et al., 4th edition). Order statistics and statistical quality control, however, continue to use it. If A & B are the greatest & smallest observation in distribution. The Range is given by

$$Range = X_{max} - X_{min}$$
$$Coefficient\ of\ Range = \frac{X_{max} - X_{min}}{X_{max} + X_{min}}$$

4.3.1.2 Computation of Range for Ungrouped Data

The formula to find the range of ungrouped data or discrete distribution of data is given as:

Range = Highest value of the data set – Lowest value of the data set

4.3.1.3 Computation of Range of Grouped Data

In the case of continuous frequency distribution or grouped data, the range is defined as the difference between the upper limit of the maximum interval of the grouped data and the lower limit of the minimum interval. It is the simplest measure of dispersion (A.K. Sharma et al., 2005). It gives a comprehensive view of the total spread of the observations. Thus, the formula to calculate the range of a grouped data is given below:

Range = Upper-class boundary of the highest interval – Lower class boundary of the lowest interval

4.3.1.4 Computation of Range for Ungrouped Data/Individual Series

Calculate the range and coefficient of range for the following data values.

45, 55, 63, 76, 67, 84, 75, 48, 62, 65

Sol. Let Xi values be: 45, 55, 63, 76, 67, 84, 75, 48, 62, 65

Here,

Maxium value (X_{max}) = 84

Minimum or Least value (X_{min}) = 45

Range = Maximum value = Minimum value = 84 – 45 = 39

$$\text{Coefficient of Range} = \frac{X_{max} - X_{min}}{X_{max} + X_{min}}$$

$$= \frac{(84 - 45)}{(84 + 45)}$$

$$= \frac{39}{129}$$

$$= 0.302$$

Example: Find the range and coefficient of range of the following data

X	3	4	5	6	7	8	9	10
Frequency	35	30	20	10	6	3	2	1

Sol. $\text{Range} = X_{max} - X_{min} = 10 - 3 = 7$

$$\text{Coefficient of Range} = \frac{X_{max} - X_{min}}{X_{max} + X_{min}}$$

$$= \frac{10-3}{10+3} = \frac{7}{13} = 0.53$$

Example: Age (in years) of 6 boys and 6 girls are recorded as below:

Girls	6	7	9	8	10	10
boys	7	9	12	14	13	17

(a) Find the range for each group.

(b) Find the range if the two groups are combined together.

Sol. a) The range for group of girls = 10 − 6 = 4

The range for group of boys = 17 − 7 = 10

(b) If the ages of the group of boys and girls are combined, then the range will be:

17 − 4 = 13

4.3.1.5 Computation of Range for Grouped Data

Example: Find the range and coefficient of range of the following data

C-I	5-10	10-15	15-20	20-25	25-30	30-35
Frequency	6	11	19	4	3	1

Solution:
$$\text{Range} = X_{max} - X_{min} = 35 - 5 = 30$$

$$\text{Coefficient of Range} = \frac{X_{max} - X_{min}}{X_{max} + X_{min}}$$

$$= \frac{35 - 5}{35 + 5} = \frac{30}{40} = 0.75$$

Example: Find out the range for the following frequency distribution table for the marks scored by class 10 students.

C-I	0-10	10-20	20-30	30-40
Frequency	5	8	15	9

Solution:
$$\text{Range} = X_{max} - X_{min} = 40 - 0 = 40$$

$$\text{Coefficient of Range} = \frac{X_{max} - X_{min}}{X_{max} + X_{min}}$$

$$= \frac{40 - 0}{40 + 0} = \frac{40}{40} = 1$$

4.3.1.6 Merits or Uses:

➢ It is the simplest to comprehend, even for a novice, and the easiest to compute. It is among the measurements that are defined by stiffness. With only one look, it provides us with the complete image of the issue.

➢ For quality control, it is used to assess a product's quality. In order to preserve quality when creating R-charts, range is crucial.

- ➢ Additionally, the range of prices over the last few periods is taken into consideration when determining the price of gold and shares.
- ➢ Additionally, by considering the range of temperatures, the Meteorological Department anticipates the weather.

4.3.1.7 Demerits or Limitations or Drawbacks

- ➢ Not all terms are used to determine range. Its size is reflected only in extreme goods. Because the range ignores all other middle values, it cannot be a perfect representation of the data.
- ➢ The aforementioned reason makes range an unreliable indicator of dispersion. Even if every other variable and word in between is altered, the range remains unchanged.
- ➢ Sampling fluctuation affects range too much. Each sample has a different range. The range grows as the sample size does, and the other way around.

4.3.3 Quartile Deviation (QD)

We need an additional measure of variability because many of the data's values fall somewhere in the middle of the frequency distribution, and range is dependent on the extremes (outliers) of a distribution. The Quartile Deviation is a straightforward method for calculating a distribution's spread around a metric representing its central tendency, typically the mean. The range that the middle 50% of your sample data falls inside is so indicated. The Coefficient of Quartile Deviation can therefore be derived based on the quartile deviation, making it simple to compare the spread of two or more distinct distributions.

4.3.2.1 What is Quartile Deviation?

A dataset that has already been sorted is split in half by a median. Similarly, a dataset is split into four equal parts using the quartiles. As a result, a given distribution should theoretically have three quartiles, but if you think about it, the second quartile is actually equal to the median! In this section, we will address the remaining two quartiles.

- ➢ The value that falls midway between the median and the lowest value in the distribution (when it is already sorted in ascending order) is known as the first quartile, lower quartile, or 25th percentile, and is also represented by the letter Q1. As a result, it indicates the area that contains 25% of the original data.

- ➢ Similarly, when the distribution is already sorted in ascending order, the value that falls halfway between the median and the highest value is known as the third quartile, upper quartile, or 75th percentile, and is also represented by the letter Q3. Consequently, it denotes the area that contains 75% of the original data or 25% of the final data.

4.3.2.2 Definition of Quartile Deviation

According to Garret (1966): the Quartile deviation is half the scale distance between 75th and 25th percent in a frequency distribution. The entire data is divided into fourmequal parts and each part contains 25% of the values.

According to Guilford (1963): the Semi-Interquartile range is the one half the range of the middle 50 percent of the cases

On the basis of above definitions, it can be said that quartile deviation is half the distance between Q1 and Q3.

4.3.2.3 The interquartile range, or IQR, is the range calculated for the middle 50% of the distribution. It is determined by taking the lower quartile (Q1) and upper quartile (Q3), or Q3–Q1. Extreme values have no effect on IQR.

4.3.2.4 Quartile Deviation (QD) or Semi-Interquartile Range (SIQR): Semi-interquartile range refers to half of the IQR. Another name for SIQR is quartile deviation, or QD.

QD is therefore calculated as

$$Q.D = \frac{(Q_3 - Q_1)}{2}$$

Where,

Q_3 = Upper Quartile (Size of $3\left[\frac{N+1}{4}\right]^{th}$ item)

Q_1 = Lower Quartile (Size of $\left[\frac{N+1}{4}\right]^{th}$ item)

Therefore, dividing IQR by 2 yields the quartile deviation. Quartile deviation, which is stated in the same unit as scores, is an absolute measure of dispersion.

Since the median responds to the number of scores that fall below it rather than to their precise locations, and because Q1 and Q3 are defined similarly, the quantile deviation and median are closely connected. The median and Common characteristics are shared by quartile deviation. The quartile deviation and median are unaffected by extreme numbers. Q1 = Q3-Median, or the two quartiles Q1 and Q3 are equally spaced from the median in a symmetrical distribution. Therefore, similar to the median, the quartile deviation encompasses precisely 50% of the data's observed values. The quartile deviation is known as the PE, or probable error, in a normal distribution. The only plausible measure of variability to calculate if the distribution is open-class is the quartile deviation.
Q1 and Q3 are not equally spaced from Q2 or the median in an asymmetric or skewed distribution. The median of the IQR shifts in the direction of the skewed tail in such a distribution. One can

evaluate the degree and direction of skewness using relative distance between Q1, Q2, and Q3 as well as the quartile deviation

4.3.2.5 Computation of Quartile Deviation for Ungrouped Data

For an ungrouped data, quartiles can be obtained using the following formulas,

$$Q_1 = \left[\frac{N+1}{4}\right]^{th} \text{item}$$

$$Q_2 = \left[\frac{N+1}{2}\right]^{th} \text{item}$$

$$Q_3 = \left[\frac{3(N+1)}{4}\right]^{th} \text{item}$$

Where n represents the total number of observations in the given data set.
Also, Q_2 is the median of the given data set, Q_1 is the median of the lower half of the data set and Q_3 is the median of the upper half of the data set.
Before estimating the quartiles, we have to arrange the given data values in ascending order.
If the value of n is even, we can follow the similar procedure of finding the median.

4.3.2.6 Computation of Quartile Deviation for Grouped Data
For a grouped data, the quartiles can be calculated using the following formula:

$$Q_1 = l + \frac{\left(\frac{N}{4} - cf\right)}{f} \times h$$

$$Q_3 = l + \frac{\left(\frac{3N}{4} - cf\right)}{f} \times h$$

Here n is for the particular quartile,

N is the total frequency,

f is the frequency of the particular class,

cf is the cumulative frequency of the preceding class,

h is the common difference,

4.3.2.7 Coefficient of Quartile Deviation

In order to compare the variability of two or more series with different units, it is necessary to determine the relative measure of Quartile Deviation, also known as the Coefficient of Quartile Deviation. This is because Quartile Deviation is an absolute measure of dispersion, and it cannot be used to compare the variability of two or more distributions when they are expressed in different units. It is studied to compare the degree of variation in different series. The formula for calculating the Coefficient of Quartile Deviation is as follows:

$$Coefficient\ of\ Q.D = \left(\frac{Q_3 - Q_1}{Q_3 + Q_1}\right)$$

Where,

Q_3 = Upper Quartile

Q_1 = Lower Quartile

- ➢ The extreme extremes of the distribution are not taken into consideration by the Quartile Deviation. As a result, only the central 50% of the data is taken into account.

- ➢ If the scale of the data is changed, the Qd also changes in the same ratio.

- ➢ For open-ended systems with open-ended extreme ranges, it is the most effective dispersion metric.

- ➢ Additionally, compared to the range (an additional measure of dispersion), it is less impacted by sampling changes in the dataset. Because it depends only on the distribution's center values, any experiment with anomalous or erroneous values would have a significant impact on the outcome.

4.3.2.8 Example to find out QD in case of Individual Series:

Example: With the help of the data given below, find the interquartile range, quartile deviation, and coefficient of quartile deviation.

150,100,268,280,195,140,200

Solution: First, we have to arrange the data into Ascending order

100,140,150,195,200,268,280

$$Q_1 = \left[\frac{N+1}{4}\right]^{th} item = 2^{nd}\ item$$

$$Q_1 = 140$$

$$Q_3 = \left[\frac{3(N+1)}{4}\right]^{th} item = 6^{th} \text{ item}$$

$$Q_3 = 268$$

Interquartile Range $= Q_3 - Q_1 = 268 - 140 = 128$

Quartile Deviation $= Q.D = \frac{(Q3 - Q1)}{2} = 64$

$$Coefficient\ of\ Q.D = \left(\frac{Q_3 - Q_1}{Q_3 + Q_1}\right) = 0.31$$

4.3.2.9 Example to find out QD in case of Discrete Series:

Example: Find Quartile and Quartile deviation of the following discrete Frequency distribution?

Items	50	55	60	65	70	75
Frequency	12	15	20	2	6	9

Solution.**Table for the calculation of Calculation of Quartile deviation**

X	Frequency	CF
50	12	12
55	15	27
60	20	47
65	2	49
70	6	55
75	9	64
	$\sum f_i = 64$	

$$Q_1 = \left[\frac{N+1}{4}\right]^{th} item = \left[\frac{64+1}{4}\right]^{th} = 16.2$$

$$Q_1 = 55$$

$$Q_3 = \left[\frac{3(N+1)}{4}\right]^{th} item = \left[\frac{3(64+1)}{4}\right]^{th} = 48.7$$

$$Q_3 = 65$$

4.3.2.10 Example to find out QD in case of Continuous Series:

Example: Find Quartile and Quartile deviation of the following Continous Frequency distribution?

C-I	0-10	10-20	20-30	30-40	40-50
freq	4	15	28	16	7

Solution:

Table for the calculation of Calculation of Quartile deviation

C-I	f	CF
0-10	4	4
10-20	15	19
20-30	28	47
30-40	16	63
40-50	7	70

$$Q_1 = \frac{N}{4} = \frac{70}{4} = 17.5, \quad Q_3 = \frac{3N}{4} = \frac{3\times70}{4} = 52.5$$

$$Q_1 = l + \frac{\left(\frac{N}{4} - cf\right)}{f} \times h = 10 + \frac{\left(\frac{70}{4} - 4\right)}{15} \times 10 = 10 + \frac{(13.5 - 4)}{15} \times 10 = 19$$

$$Q_3 = l + \frac{\left(\frac{3N}{4} - cf\right)}{f} \times h = 30 + \frac{\left(\frac{3 \times 70}{4} - 47\right)}{f} \times 10 = 30 + \frac{(52.5 - 47)}{16} \times 10$$

$$Q_3 = 30 + \frac{(5.5)}{16} \times 10 = 33.43$$

$$Q.D = \frac{(Q_3 - Q_1)}{2} = Q.D = \frac{(33.43 - 19)}{2} = 7.215$$

$$Coefficient\ of\ Q.D = \left(\frac{Q_3 - Q_1}{Q_3 + Q_1}\right) = \left(\frac{33.43 - 19}{33.43 + 19}\right) = 0.275$$

4.3.2.11 Importance of Quartile Deviation

Data, frequency, and trend distribution can all be better understood with the use of statistics. In the frequency distribution table, the difference between the first and third quartiles is known as the quartile deviation (Mohanty et al., 2016). This is sometimes referred to as the interquartile range. Because many regressions and deviations that aid in evaluating the properties of the data may be computed within this range, it is significant. Quartile deviation or semi-interquartile range is the term used to describe the result of dividing the interquartile range by two.

4.3.2.12 Merits and Limitations of Quartile Deviation

1. Compared to range, which is based on the greatest and lowest values of the data, quantile deviation accounts for 50% of the data, making it a more accurate indicator of dispersion.
2. Second, because the quartile deviation does not take into account 25% of the data at the start and 25% at the conclusion, it is unaffected by extreme scores.
3. Finally, the only dispersion metric that can be calculated from the frequency distribution using an open-end class is the quartile deviation.

Despite the major merits of quartile deviation, there are limitations to it as well.

1. The quartile deviation value is not based on all observations; rather, it is based on the middle 50% readings. As a result, it is not thought of as a reliable indicator of variability.
2. Sampling variability affects the quartile deviation value.

3. The distribution of the individual values within the intervals of the middle 50% observed values has no bearing on the quartile deviation value.

4.3.2.13 Uses of Quartile Deviation

1. There are relatively few and extremely severe scores in the distribution.
2. When central tendency is measured by the median.
3. When figuring out the concentration around the median is our main goal.

4.3.4   Mean Deviation

As you are aware, a measure of dispersion should be based on all objects, which is one of its properties. According to this perspective, range and quartile deviations are not optimal since they do not take into account all of the data's observations. However, since the mean (or average) deviation metric is based on every observation in the provided data set, it is excellent in this regard. The arithmetic mean of the absolute deviations of each individual observation from the average of the provided data is used to calculate this metric. Although the mode can occasionally be utilized, the mean or median is the average that is commonly employed to calculate the mean deviation. Absolute deviations indicate that, regardless of their actual sign, the deviations are seen as positive. Its definition is the mean of the observations' absolute deviation from any central tendency measure.

4.3.3.1 What is Mean Deviation

In statistics, deviation is a metric used to describe the discrepancy between a variable's observed and predicted values. To put it simply, a deviation is the distance from the center. The center points of a data collection are the mean, median, and mode. The distance between the values in a data collection and the center point is also determined using the mean deviation.

A statistical metric called mean deviation calculates the average departure from the mean value of a certain set of data. Numerous data series, including continuous, discrete, and individual data series, can be used to compute the mean deviation.

4.3.3.2 Mean Deviation Formula

The mean of the absolute departures of the data or observations from a suitable average is known as the mean deviation. The mean, median, or mode might be this appropriate average. It is sometimes referred to as the mean absolute deviation.

4.3.3.3 Computation of Mean Deviation about mean for Ungrouped Data

The basic formula to calculate mean deviation for a given data set is as follows:

$$M.D = \frac{\sum |X_i - \bar{X}|}{N}$$

$x_i = x_1, x_2, \ldots \ldots x_n$
$\bar{x} = mean\ of\ observation$

4.3.3.4 Computation of Mean Deviation about mean for Discrete Series

$$M.D = \frac{\sum f |X_i - \bar{X}|}{N}$$

$x_i = x_1, x_2, \ldots \ldots x_n$
$f_i = f_1, f_2, \ldots \ldots f_n$
$N = sum\ of\ frequencies$

4.3.3.5 Computation of Mean Deviation about mean for Continuous Series

$$M.D = \frac{\sum f |X_i - \bar{X}|}{N}$$

$x_i = mid\ point\ of\ class\ interval$
$f_i = f_1, f_2, \ldots \ldots f_n$
$N = sum\ of\ frequencies$

4.3.3.6 Computation of Mean Deviation about median for Ungrouped Data

$$M.D = \frac{\sum |X_i - Md|}{N}$$

$x_i = x_1, x_2, \ldots \ldots x_n\ observation$
$Md = median\ of\ observation$

4.3.3.7 Computation of Mean Deviation about median for Grouped Data

$$M.D = \frac{\sum f |X_i - Md|}{N}$$

$x_i = x_1, x_2, \ldots \ldots x_n$
$f_i = f_1, f_2, \ldots \ldots f_n$
$N = sum\ of\ frequencies$

4.3.3.8 Computation of Mean Deviation about mean for Continuous Series

$$M.D = \frac{\sum f|X_i - Md|}{N}$$

$x_i = mid\ point\ of\ class\ interval$
$f_i = f_1, f_2, \dots \dots f_n$
$N = sum\ of\ frequencies$

Coefficient of M.D about Median $= \dfrac{M.D.\ Median}{Median}$

Similarly, a coefficient of M. D about Mean $= \dfrac{(M.D.\ about\ \bar{X})}{Mean}$

4.3.3.9 Example to find out MD in case of Discrete Series:

Find Mean deviation about mean and Median for following data in case of discrete series?
X: 6,7,10,12,13,4,8,12

Solution: first we have to find out mean then put it to the formula of Mean deviation about Mean.
i.e $M.D = \dfrac{\sum |X_i - \bar{X}|}{N}$

Table for the calculation of Calculation of Mean deviation about Mean

X	$|X_i - \bar{X}|$
6	$|6 - 9| = 3$
7	2
10	1
12	3
13	4
4	5
8	1
12	3
	$\sum |X_i - \bar{X}| = 22$

$$\bar{X} = \frac{\sum X_i}{N} = \frac{72}{8} = 9$$

$$M.D = \frac{\sum |X_i - \bar{X}|}{N} = \frac{22}{7} = 2.75$$

Now we have to find out Mean deviation about Median
First we have to arrange the data into ascending order, then find out the Median first

$X = 4,6,7,8,10,12,12,13$

$$M.D = \frac{\frac{N}{2} + \frac{N}{2} + 1}{2} = 9$$

Table for the calculation of Calculation of Mean deviation about Median

X	$|X_i - Md|$
6	3
7	2
10	1
12	3
13	4
4	5
8	1
12	3
	=22

$$M.D = \frac{\sum |X_i - Md|}{N} = 2.75$$

4.3.3.10 Example to find out MD in case of Continuous Series:

Example: Calculate Mean deviation about Mean?

C-I	0-10	10-20	20-30	30-40	40-50	50-60	60-70
Freq	6	5	8	15	7	6	3

Solution: In the case first we have to find out Mean

$$\bar{X} = A + \frac{\Sigma f d_i}{N} \times h$$

$$\bar{X} = 35 + \frac{(-8)}{50} \times 10 = 33.4$$

After Finding Mean we have to the value of mean in the formula of Mean deviation about Mean

$$M.D = \frac{\Sigma f_i |X_i - \bar{X}|}{N} = \frac{659.2}{50} = 13.18$$

Table for the calculation of Calculation of Mean deviation about Mean

C-I	f	X	$d_i = \frac{X_i - h}{h}$	fd	$|X_i - \bar{X}|$	$f|X_i - \bar{X}|$
0-10	6	5	-3	-18	5-33.4=28.4	170.4
10-20	5	15	-2	-10	18.4	92
20-30	8	25	-1	-8	8.4	67.2
30-40	15	35	0	0	1.6	24
40-50	7	45	1	7	11.6	81.2
50-60	6	55	2	2	21.6	129.6
60-70	3	65	3	9	31.6	94.8
	N=50					$\sum f|X_i - \bar{X}| = 659.2$

4.3.3.11 Merits and Limitations of the Mean Deviation

The following are MD's primary advantages:

1) MD is simple to calculate and comprehend.
2) Unlike R or QD, it is based on all observations.
3) Because it averages the absolute deviations, it provides a precise indicator of variability.
4) Extreme observations have less of an impact.
5) Because it is based on average, it is a more useful metric for comparing how various distributions form.

The following are average deviation's primary drawbacks:
1) We treat all numbers as positive and disregard the plus-minus sign when computing average deviation. Due to this mathematical characteristic, it is Inferential statistics do not use it.
2) For open-end classes, AD cannot be calculated.
3) It tends to rise as sample size increases.

4.3.3.12 Uses of Mean Deviation

Economists and business statisticians utilize AD or MD despite its drawbacks. It is also employed in determining how individual wealth is distributed within a community or a country. The National Bureau of Economic Research claims that for this reason, MD is the most useful dispersion metric (Mohanty and Misra, 2016, pg. 133).

1) When all deviations from the mean are to be weighted based on their magnitude.
2) When the existence of extreme scores unreasonably affects the standard deviation.
3) The score distribution is not nearly typical.

4.3.4 Standard Deviation (SD)

The standard deviation, a key idea in statistics, quantifies the dispersion of data points and indicates how far a dataset's data points depart from the mean, giving an obvious idea of the data's variability or spread (Cureton, E. E. 1968). Finding the deviation of a data value from the mean value, or the dispersion of all the values in a data collection to the mean value, is done using the standard deviation formula. A random variable's standard deviation can be determined using a variety of standard deviation formulas (Bolch et al., 1968).

4.3.4.1 Standard Deviation in Statistics

The degree of dispersion of the data point from the mean value is known as the standard deviation. It provides information on the variation of the data points in the data sample as well as how their values differ from their mean values (Holtzman et al., 1950).
Standard Deviation of a given sample of data set is also defined as the square root of the variance of the data set.

When we have n number of observations and the observations are $x_1, x_2 \ldots \ldots x_n$, then the mean deviation of the value from the mean is determined as $\sum_{i=1}^{n}(x_i - \bar{x})^2$. Nevertheless, it does not appear that the sum of squares of departures from the mean is a reliable indicator of dispersion. A tiny average of the squared deviations from the mean suggests that the observations x_i are near the average $\bar{x}$. This dispersion level is lower. If this total is big, it suggests that the observations are more widely distributed from the mean $\bar{x}$. Thus we conclude that $\sum_{i=1}^{n}(x_i - \bar{x})^2$ is a reasonable indicator of the degree of dispersion or scatter. We take $\sum_{i=1}^{n}(x_i - \bar{x})^2$ as a proper measure of dispersion and this is called the variance (σ^2). The positive square root of the variance is the standard deviation.

4.3.4.2 Standard Deviation Formula

Data sets can be classified as either populations or samples. A population comprises all the members in the group that we are interested in researching, whereas a sample is a subset of the population. There is some variation in the formulas used to compute the population and sample standard deviations.

The population standard deviation formula is given as:

$$\sigma = \sqrt{\frac{1}{N}\sum_{i=1}^{N}(X_i - \mu)^2} = \sqrt{\frac{1}{N}\sum d_i^{\,2}}$$

Here,

σ = Population standard deviation symbol

μ = Population mean

N = total number of observations

Similarly, the sample standard deviation formula is:

$$s = \sqrt{\frac{1}{n-1}\sum_{i=1}^{n}(x_i - \bar{x})^2}$$

Here,

s = Sample standard deviation symbol

$\bar{x}$ = Arithmetic mean of the observations

n = total number of observations

4.3.4.3 Computation of Standard Deviation in case of Discrete Series and shortcut Method

$$\sigma = \sqrt{\frac{\sum d_i^{\,2}}{N} - \left(\frac{\sum d_i}{N}\right)^2}$$

σ = Population standard deviation

N = Number of observations in population

$d_i = X_i - A$

4.3.4.4 Computation of Standard Deviation in case of Continuous Series

$$\sigma = \sqrt{\frac{\Sigma f d_i^2}{N} - \left(\frac{\Sigma f d_i}{N}\right)^2}$$

σ = Population standard deviation

N = Number of observations in population

$d_i = X_i - A$

f is the frequency

4.3.4.5 Variance: The square of the deviation is called variance and is given by

$$\sigma^2 = \frac{1}{N} \sum f_i (X_i - \bar{X})^2$$

σ = Population standard deviation

N = Number of observations in population

$X_i = i^{th}$ observation in the population

$\bar{X}$ = Population mean

4.3.4.6 Example to find out Standard Deviation in case of Discrete Series:

Example: Calculate Standard deviation by direct method for individual series?

X: 40,44,54,60,62,64,90,96

Solution: First we have to find out the Mean of the observation

$$\bar{X} = \frac{\Sigma X_i}{N} = 63.75$$

Table for the calculation of Calculation of Standard deviation

X	$d_x = X_i - \bar{X}$	$d^2{}_x = (X_i - \bar{X})^2$
40	40-63.75=23.75	564.062
44	19.75	390.062
54	9.75	95.06
60	3.75	14.06
62	1.75	3.06
64	0.25	0.062
90	26.25	689.06
96	32.25	1040.062
		$\sum d_i{}^2 = 2795.488$

Then put all the value in the standard deviation formula and we will get the value of σ

$$\sigma = \sqrt{\frac{\sum d_x{}^2}{N}} = \sqrt{\frac{2795.48}{8}} = 18.69$$

Hence standard deviation for this data is 18.69

Example: In a class of 50, 4 students were selected at random and their total marks in the final assessments are recorded, which are: 812, 836, 982, and 769. Find the variance and standard deviation of their marks.

Solution: n = 4

Sample Mean $(\bar{X}) = \frac{(812+836+982+769)}{4} = 849.75$

Here also, we have to calculate the sample standard deviation as the given data is just a sample.

$$\text{Variance} = \sigma^2 = \frac{1}{n-1}\sum(x_i - \bar{x})^2 = \frac{1}{3}\sum(x_i - 849.75)^2$$

$$= \frac{(812 - 849.75)^2 + (836 - 849.75)^2 + (982 - 849.75)^2 + (769 - 849.75)^2}{3}$$

$$= 8541.58$$

Using the SD formula,

$$\sigma = \sqrt{8541.58} = 92.4$$

Variance is 8541.58 and standard deviation for this data is 92.4

Example: Calculate Standard deviation by shortcut method?

X: 40, 44, 54, 60, 62, 64, 70, 80

Solution: In case of short cut mean we have to find out $d_i = X_i - A$

Table for the calculation of Calculation of Standard deviation

X	$d_i = X_i - A$	d_i^2
40	40-60=-20	400
44	-16	256
54	-6	36
60=A	0	0
62	2	4
64	4	16
70	10	100

80	20	400
	$\sum d_i = -6$	$\sum d_i^2 = 1212$

After finding the value of $\sum d_i^2$ and $\sum d_i$ then put all these value in the formula of standard deviation then we will get the value of σ

$$\sigma = \sqrt{\frac{\sum d_i^2}{N} - \left(\frac{\sum d_i}{N}\right)^2}$$

$$= \sqrt{\frac{1212}{8} - \left(\frac{-6}{8}\right)^2}$$

$$= \sqrt{151.5 - 0.6}$$

$$= 12.24$$

Hence standard deviation for this data is 12.24

4.3.4.7 Example to find out Standard Deviation in case of Continuous Series:

Example: Calculate Standard deviation for the following data?

C-I	10-20	20-30	30-40	40-50	50-60	60-70
freq	2	4	8	10	12	4

Solution: For finding the value of standard deviation, first we have to find out the value

$d_i = X - A$ and then find out the value of $\sum f d_i$ and all the value which is required in the formula

Table for the calculation of Calculation of Standard deviation

C-I	f	X_i	$d_i = X - A$	fd_i	d_i^2	fd_i^2
10-20	2	15	15-35=-20	2*-20=-40	400	800
20-30	4	25	=-10	-40	100	400
30-40	8	35=A	0	0	0	0
40-50	10	45	10	100	100	1000
50-60	12	55	20	240	400	4800
60-70	4	65	30	120	900	3600
	n=40			$\sum fd_i = 380$		=10600

$$\sigma = \sqrt{\frac{\sum fd_i^2}{N} - \left(\frac{\sum fd_i}{N}\right)^2} = \sqrt{\frac{10600}{40} - \left(\frac{380}{40}\right)^2} = 13.21$$

Question for Practice

Q: Find the range and coefficient of range of the following data.

X   43.5, 13.6, 18.9, 38.4, 61.4, 29.8

Ans: 47.3, 0.64

Q: Calculate the quartile deviation for the following distribution?

C-I	0-10	10-20	20-30	30-40	40-50	50-60	60-70	70-80	80-90	90-100

f	5	3	4	3	3	4	7	9	7	8

Ans. 24.16

Q The rainfall recorded in various places of five districts in a week are given below. Find its standard deviation.

Rainfall(in mm)	45	50	55	60	65	70
freq	5	13	4	9	5	4

Ans 7.76

4.3.4.8 Merits of Standard Deviation

1. It has no ambiguity and is precisely defined.
2. It cannot be accurately estimated by omitting any of the series' items because it is predicated on all of the observations in the series.
3. It never disregards the + and - signs, such as the mean deviation, and adheres rigorously to algebraic rules.
4. Because of its many algebraic features, it can be further treated algebraically.
   In advanced statistical analysis, such as regression, skewness, correlation, and sample studies, it is a powerful tool.
5. It is frequently used to test hypotheses and perform various tests of significance, such as the t^2 test and others, and is not significantly impacted by sample fluctuations.

4.3.4.9 Demerits of Standard Deviation

1. The average person does not understand it.
2. Because it incorporates numerous mathematical models and procedures, its computation is challenging.
3. Insofar as the squares of deviations of large items are proportionately larger than the squares of the smaller items, it is greatly influenced by the extreme values of a series.
4. The dispersion of two or more series presented in different units cannot be compared using it.

4.3.4.10 Standard Deviation vs. Variance

The statistics of variance and standard deviation are connected. By taking the mean of the data points, removing the mean from each data point separately, squaring each result, and then taking another mean of these squares, this variance can be calculated. The variance's square root is the standard deviation (Pearson et al., 1970).
When compared to the mean value, variance aids in determining the spread size of the data. More variety in data values and sometimes a wider gap between data values emerge as the variance increases. The variance will be lower if all of the data values are near to one another. However, because variances indicate a squared result that might not be usefully expressed on the same graph as the original dataset, they are more challenging to understand than the standard deviation.
Generally speaking, standard deviations are simpler to visualize and use. While the variance isn't always expressed in the same unit of measurement as the data, the standard deviation is. A normal curve or other mathematical relationship in the data can be ascertained by statisticians using the standard deviation (Holtzman et al., 1950)..

The average, or mean, data point will be within one standard deviation of 68% of the data points if the data behaves as a normal curve. A greater number of data points deviate from the standard deviation when the variance is larger. There is more data that is around average when the variances are smaller (Markowitch et al.,1968).

4.4 Conclusion

In conclusion, data cannot be adequately described by central tendency measures alone. Therefore, we need to give a measure of variability or dispersion in order to properly characterize distribution (McBride et al., 2018). The variability measures are condensed numbers that quantitatively describe how much a distribution's scores cluster or disperse around one another. Range, quartile deviation, average deviation, standard deviation, and variance are the metrics used to quantify variability. Range is helpful for preliminary work and is simple to compute (Kendall et al., 1977).. However, this solely takes into account severe items and ignores intermediate scores. As a result, it is useless as a descriptive metric. The median has a relationship with quantile deviation in its attributes. The amount of scores that fall above or below the outer quartile point is taken into account, but not their quantity. With open-ended distribution, this is helpful. The average deviation considers the precise where each score falls inside the distribution. Although it is mathematically insufficient, the means deviation provides a more accurate indication of the range of scores. The sample volatility has less of an impact on the average deviation (Minium et al.,2001). The most reliable indicator of variability is the standard deviation. The standard deviation indicates the degree to which the score deviates from the mean. The original scores unit is used to express it. As a result, it is the variability measure that descriptive statistics employ the most. The arithmetic mean of the squared deviations of each individual score is known as the variance (σ^2) or mean square (MS).

Chapter 5: Skewness (The extent of symmetry/asymmetry) and Kurtosis (The flatness or peaked ness)

A statistics metric called skewness evaluates how asymmetrical a probability distribution is. It measures how much the data is moved to one side or skewed. A longer tail on the right side of the distribution is indicated by positive skewness, and a longer tail on the left side is indicated by negative skewness. Skewness aids in comprehending a dataset's form and outliers (Elhance et al., 1988). Skewness, a statistical measure of asymmetry, is exhibited by a probability distribution that differs from the symmetrical normal distribution (bell curve) in a given collection of data.

5.1 What is Skewness?

Skewness is a statistical metric that characterizes the absence of symmetry or asymmetry in a dataset's probability distribution. It measures the extent to which the data differs from a distribution that is exactly symmetrical, like a normal distribution (bell-shaped). Because it sheds light on the distributional form and characteristics of a dataset, skewness is a useful statistical concept. Understanding whether a dataset is positively or negatively skewed, for instance, can be crucial in a variety of industries, such as finance, economics, and data analysis, since it can affect how data is interpreted and which statistical methods are used (Yule, G U. et al., 1991).

The normal distribution aids in determining skewness. Symmetrically distributed data is referred to as having a normal distribution. The symmetrical distribution is skewless. since all central tendency measures fall within the middle.

A dataset that is symmetrically distributed has an equal number of observations on the left and right sides. In the event that the dataset has 90 values, there are 45 observations on the left and 45 on the right. However, what if the distribution isn't symmetrical? Time skewness enters the picture, and the data is referred to as asymmetrical data.

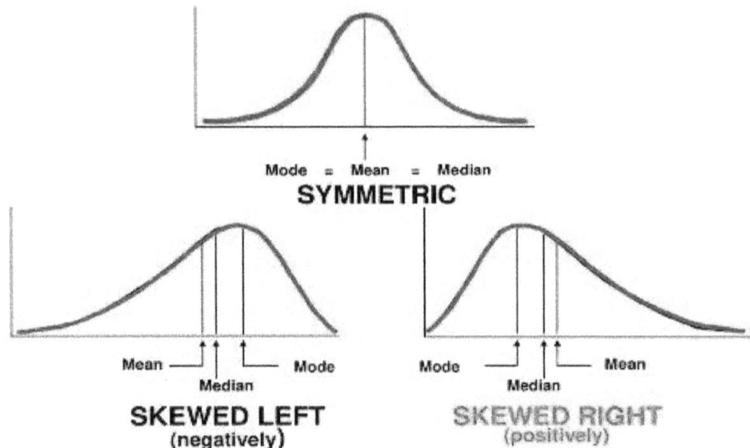

Figure 5.1: Symmetrical distribution and non-symmetrical distribution

5.2 Tests of Skewness

A dataset's skewness can be evaluated using a variety of statistical tests and techniques. You can use these tests to find out if a dataset is roughly symmetric, negatively skewed, or positively skewed (Yule, G U et al., 1991). The following are some typical methods and tests for determining skewness:

1. **Visual Inspection:** Making a density plot or histogram out of the provided data is the most straightforward method of determining skewness. A plot is said to be negatively skewed if it is skewed to the left, and positively skewed if it is slanted to the right. The plot has no skewness if it is approximately symmetrical.

2. **Skewness Coefficient (Pearson's First Coefficient of Skewness):** This is a numerical measure of skewness, which determines the skewness when mean and mode are not equal. It is calculated as:

   Skewness as per Karl Pearson's Measure = Mean – Mode

3. **Quartiles are not equidistant** from each other; i.e., $Q3-Me \neq Me-Q1$.

5.3 Positive and Negative Skewness

The distribution of a dataset might diverge from perfect symmetry (a normal distribution) in two ways: positively and negatively. They explain which way the data is skewed or asymmetrical.

5.3.1 Positive Skewness (Right Skew): When a distribution is positively skewed, the larger values on the right side of the tail are longer than the smaller values on the left. This indicates that there are some extreme values on the right side of the distribution, while the majority of data points are centered on the left. When a dataset is favorably skewed,

$$\text{Mean} > \text{Median} > \text{Mode}$$

The distribution of income (most people earn a moderate income, but some earn extremely high incomes), exam results (most students score in a certain range, but some score exceptionally high), and stock market returns (most days have modest returns, but a few days may have very high returns) are examples of positively skewed data.

5.3.2 Negative Skewness (Left Skew)

The tail on the left, which represents the smaller values, is longer than the tail on the right, which represents the larger values, in a distribution that is negatively skewed. This suggests that there are a few extreme values on the left side of the distribution, while the majority of the data points are concentrated on the right side. When a dataset is negatively skewed,

$$\text{Mean} < \text{Median} < \text{Mode}$$

The age at retirement (where most people retire at a certain age, but a few retire exceptionally early), test scores on an easy test (where most students score well, but a few score very low), and the gestational age at birth (where most babies are born full-term, but a few are born prematurely) are examples of negatively skewed data.

The forms of both negatively and positively skewed distributions are shown in Fig. 5.1. There are several methods for quantifying the degree and direction of skewness. In this unit, we'll talk about four skewness metrics.

5.3.3 Zero Skewness (Symmetrical Distribution)

When the mean, median, and mode are all equal, the distribution is said to be perfectly symmetrical when the skewness is zero. The data points are uniformly spaced around the central point in a symmetrical distribution.

An example would be a dataset that is perfectly balanced, with equal frequencies for each value.

5.4 Various Measurement of Skewness

Both absolute and relative skewness measures are possible. Since the mean, median, and mode of a symmetrical distribution are all the same, the more the mean deviates from the mode, the greater the asymmetry or skewness. Since the same quantity of skewness has different implications in distributions with limited variance and distributions with big variation, an absolute measure of skewness cannot be used for comparison.

5.4.1 Absolute Measures of Skewness
Following are the absolute measures of skewness:
1. Skewness (Sk) = Mean – Median
2. Skewness (Sk) = Mean – Mode
3. Skewness (Sk) = (Q3 – Q2) – (Q2 – Q1)

For comparing to series, we do not calculate these absolute mearues we calculate the relative measures which are called coefficient of skewness. Coefficient of skewness are pure numbers independent of units of measurements.

5.4.2 Relative Measures of Skewness

We must remove the distributing influence of variation in order to compare the skewness of two or more distributions in a legitimate manner. By dividing the absolute skewness by the standard deviation, this kind of elimination can be accomplished. The key techniques for determining relative skewness are as follows:

5.4.2.1 β and γ Coefficient of Skewness

Karl Pearson defined the following β and γ coefficients of skewness, based upon the second and third central moments:

$$\beta_1 = \frac{\mu_3^2}{\mu_2^3}$$

It serves as a skewness metric. β_1 should be zero for a symmetrical distribution. As a skewness metric, β_1 does not indicate whether skewness is positive or negative. Due to the fact that μ_3, which is the sum of the cubes of the deviations from the mean, can be either positive or negative, μ_3^2 is always positive. Additionally, the variance μ_2, is always positive. Consequently, β_1 would always be positive. Karl Pearson's Gamma coefficient γ_1, which is the square root of β_1, eliminates this disadvantage. i.e.

$$\gamma_1 = \pm\sqrt{\beta_1} = \frac{\mu_3}{(\mu_2)^{\frac{3}{2}}} = \frac{\mu_3}{\sigma^3}$$

Then the sign of skewness would depend upon the value of μ_3, whether it is positive or negative. It is advisable to use γ_1 as measure of skewness.

5.4.2.2 Karl Pearson's Measure: Karl Pearson's Measure of Skewness measures the distribution's asymmetry or lack of symmetry using the mean, median, and standard deviation of the provided data set. It is a dimensionless figure that offers important information on the distributional shape of a dataset. Researchers and analysts can use this measure to better understand the direction and degree of skewness in their datasets, which can help them make better modelling and analysis decisions. It is useful in many statistical and data analysis domains (Nagar, A. L. et al.,1983).

Skewness as per Karl Pearson's Measure = Mean – Mode

Karl Pearson's Measure's Skewness
> ➤ The skewness will have a positive value if the mean is higher than the mode.
> ➤ The skewness will be negative if the mean is less than the mode.
> ➤ The skewness will be 0 when the mean and mode are equal.

Coefficient of Skewness as per Karl Pearson's Measure
> ➤ With respect to Mean and Median: $\quad S_K = \dfrac{3\times(\bar{X}-M)}{\sigma}$

> ➤ With respect to Mean and Mode: $\quad S_K = \dfrac{3\times(\bar{X}-Mode)}{\sigma}$

Here,

S_K is Karl Pearson's skewness coefficient.

$\bar{X}$ is the arithmetic mean or average of the data.

M is the middle value of the data when it is arranged in ascending order.

σ is a measure of the standard deviation of the data.

Coefficient of Karl Pearson's Measure

i.   A fully symmetric distribution, in which the data is equally distributed on both sides of the mean, is indicated if $S_K = 0$.

ii.   A positively skewed distribution with a longer or fatter tail on the right side and most of the data points concentrated on the left side of the mean is indicated if Sk > 0.

iii.   A distribution that is negatively skewed, with the majority of data points concentrated on the right side of the mean and a longer or fatter tail on the left, is indicated if Sk < 0.

A relative measure, independent of the units of measurement, is defined as the Karl Pearson's Coefficient of skewness S_K, given by

$$S_K = \frac{(Mean - Mode)}{\sigma}$$

The sign of S_K gives the direction and its magnitude gives the extent of skewness. If $S_K > 0$, the distribution is positively skewed, and if $S_K < 0$ it is negatively skewed.

The value of the Karl Pearson's coefficient of skewness usually lies between ±1 for moderately skewed distribution. If mode is not well defined, we use the formula

$$S_K = \frac{3 \times (Mean - Median)}{\sigma}$$

By using the relationship

Mode = (3 Median – 2 Mean)

Here, $-3 \leq S_K \leq 3$. In practice it is rarely obtained.

5.4.2.2.1 Computation of Karl Pearson's Measure in case of Individual Series

Calculate Pearson's skewness coefficient for a dataset of exam scores:
85, 88, 92, 94, 96, 98, 100, 100, 100, 100.

Solution:
Calculate Mean

$$Mean(\bar{X}) = \frac{\sum X_i}{N} = \frac{85, 88, 92, 94, 96, 98, 100, 100, 100, 100.}{10} = 95.3$$

Calculation of Median

Since there are 10 data points, the median is the average of the 5th and 6th values when sorted in ascending order:

$$Median = \frac{(96 + 98)}{2} = \frac{194}{2} = 97$$

Calculation of standard deviation.

$$\sigma^2 = \frac{\Sigma(xi - \mu)}{N} = \frac{(85 - 95.3)^2}{210} + \cdots + \frac{(100 - 95.3)^2}{210} = \frac{268.1}{10} = 26.81$$

$$\text{Thus, } \sigma = \sqrt{26.81}$$

$$\sigma = {\sim}5$$

Calculation of mode

It is clear from the data set that 100 is the most frequently occurring value in the data. Hence, mode of given data is 100.

Substitute the values in the formulae

A. With respect to Mean and Median: : $\quad S_K = \frac{3\times(\bar{X}-M)}{\sigma} = \frac{3\times(95.3-97)}{5} = \frac{-5}{5} = -1.02$

$$S_K = -1.02$$

B. With respect to Mean and Mode: $S_K = \frac{3\times(\bar{X}-Mode)}{\sigma} = \frac{3\times(95.3-100)}{5} = -0.94$

There is a minor negative skewness in the distribution of exam scores, as indicated by the negative skewness coefficient (S_K). This indicates that the majority of the scores are concentrated on the right side of the mean, while the distribution's tail is a little longer on the left.

5.4.2.2.2 Computation of Karl Pearson's Measure in case of Discrete Data

Example: Compute the Karl Pearson's coefficient of skewness from the following data:

Height (in inches)	58	59	60	61	62	63	64	65
Number of Persons	10	18	30	42	35	28	16	8

Solution:

Table for the computation of mean and standard deviation (s.d)

Height(X)	$U = X - 61$	Number of Persons(f)	fu	fu^2
58	-3	10	-30	90
59	-2	18	-36	72
60	-1	30	-30	30
61	0	42	0	0
62	1	35	35	35
63	2	28	56	112
64	3	16	48	144
65	4	8	32	128
Total		187		

Calculate Mean

$$Mean = 61 + \frac{75}{187} = 61.4$$

Calculation of standard deviation

$$s.d = \sqrt{\frac{611}{187} - \left(\frac{75}{187}\right)^2} = 1.76$$

Calculation of Mode

We observe that height is a continuous variable in order to determine the mode. The height is presumed to have been measured using the estimate that a height measurement that is larger than 58 but less than 58.5 inches is considered to be 58 inches, whereas a measurement that is higher than or equal to 58.5 but less than 59 inches is considered to be 59.
Thus the given data can be written as

Height(X)	Number of Persons(f)
57.5 - 58.5	10
58.5 - 59.5	18
59.5 - 60.5	30
60.5 - 61.5	42
61.5 - 62.5	35
62.5 - 63.5	28
63.5 - 64.5	16
64.5 - 65.5	**8**

By inspection, the modal class in $60.5 - 61.5$. Thus, we have

$$l = 60.5, f_1 = 42, f_2 = 35, f_0 = 30, h = 1$$

$$Mode = l + \frac{f_1 - f_0}{2f_1 - f_0 - f_2} \times h$$

$$= 60.5 + \frac{42 - 30}{2 \times 42 - 30 - 35} \times 1$$

$$= 60.5 + 0.631 = 61.131$$

$$Mode = 61.131$$

Substitute the values in the formulae, Karl Pearson's coefficient of skewness S_K, given by

$$S_K = \frac{(Mean - Mode)}{\sigma}$$

$$S_K = \frac{(61.4 - 61.131)}{1.76}$$

$$S_K = 0.153$$

Thus the distribution is positively skewed.

Example: For a distribution Karl Pearson's coefficient of skewness is 0.64, standard deviation is 13 and mean is 59.2 Find mode and median.
Solution: We have given
$S_K = 0.64$,
$\sigma = 13$ and Mean = 59.2
Therefore by using formulae

$$S_K = \frac{(Mean - Mode)}{\sigma}$$

$$0.64 = \frac{(59.2 - Mode)}{13}$$

$$Mode = 59.20 - 8.32 = 50.88$$

$$Mode = 3Median - 2Mean$$

$$50.88 = 3Median - 2(59.2)$$

$$Median = \frac{50.88 + 118.4}{3} = \frac{169.28}{3} = 56.42$$

5.4.2.3 Bowley's Measure

A statistical metric called Bowley's Skewness Coefficient, which bears the name of British economist Arthur Lyon Bowley, is used to evaluate how asymmetrical or skew a probability distribution is. Bowley's Skewness Coefficient is based on quartiles, as opposed to certain other skewness measurements that depend on moments or departures from the mean. The direction and degree of skewness in a dataset can be easily and intuitively understood thanks to this coefficient. When working with data that might not have a normal distribution or when a reliable indicator of skewness is needed, Bowley's Skewness Coefficient is very helpful (Nagar, A. L. et al., 1983).

$$S_B = \frac{Q_1 - Q_3 - 2Q_2}{Q_3 - Q_1}$$

Where,
Q_1 is the first quartile (25th percentile),
Q_2 is the second quartile (50th percentile, or median), and
Q_3 is the third quartile (75th percentile).

Coefficient of Bowley's Measure

- ➢ If B = 0, the distribution is perfectly symmetric about the mean (no skewness).
- ➢ If B < 0, the distribution is negatively skewed (left-skewed), meaning the tail on the left side of the distribution is longer or heavier.
- ➢ If B > 0, the distribution is positively skewed (right-skewed), indicating that the tail on the right side of the distribution is longer or heavier.

5.4.2.3.1 Computation of Bowley's Measure of Skewness in case of Individual Series

Example: Calculate Bowley's Measure of Skewness for the following dataset representing the ages of a group of people in a sample: 20, 24, 28, 32, 35, 40, 42, 45, 50.

Solution: **Calculate the median (Q_2)**

$Q_2 = 35$ (the middle value)

Calculate the first quartile (Q_1)

To find Q_1, $Q_1 = \frac{N+1}{4} = \frac{9+1}{4} = 2.5$
2.5th term = 2nd term + (0.5) (3rd term − 2nd term) = $24 + 0.5 \times (28 - 24)$

$$Q_1 = 26$$

Calculate the 3rd quartile (Q_3)

To find Q_3, $\qquad Q_3 = \dfrac{3(N+1)}{4} = \dfrac{3\times 10}{4} = 7.5$

7.5th term $=$ 7th term $+$ (0.5) (8th term – 7th term)

$$= 42 + 0.5 \times (45 - 42)$$
$$= 42 + 1.5$$

$$Q_3 = 43.5$$

Substitute the above values in the formula

$$S_B = \frac{Q_1 - Q_3 - 2Q_2}{Q_3 - Q_1} = \frac{26 - 43.5 - 2 \times 35}{43.5 - 26} = -0.02$$

The distribution is negatively skewed (left-skewed) because S_B is negative (B $<$ 0). This suggests that there might be outliers or high values on the right side of the data because the distribution's tail is longer on the left side.

5.4.2.3.2 Computation of Bowley's Measure of Skewness in case of Discrete Data

Let us calculate the Bowley's coefficient for the following data on height of 187 persons:

Table for the calculation of Bowley's Measure of Skewness

Height(X)	Number of Persons(f)	cf
57.5 - 58.5	10	10
58.5 - 59.5	18	28
59.5 - 60.5	30	58
60.5 - 61.5	42	100
61.5 - 62.5	35	135
62.5 - 63.5	28	163
63.5 - 64.5	16	179
64.5 - 65.5	8	187

Calculate the first quartile (Q_1)

Since $\dfrac{N}{4} = 46.75$, the first quartile class is $59.5 - 60.5$. Thus

$$Q_1 = 59.5, cf = 28, f = 30 \; and \; h = 1$$
$$\therefore Q_1 = 59.59 + \frac{46.75 - 28}{30} \times 1 = 60.125$$

Calculate the median (Q_2)

Since $\frac{N}{2} = 93.5$, the median class is $60.5 - 61.5$. Thus

$$l = 60.5, cf = 58, f = 42 \text{ and } h = 1$$

$$\therefore Q_2 = 60.5 + \frac{93 - 58}{42} \times 1 = 61.345$$

Calculate the 3rd quartile (Q_3)

Since $\frac{3N}{4} = 140.25$, the third quartile class is $62.5 - 63.5$. Thus

$$l = 62.5, cf = 135, f = 28 \text{ and } h = 1$$

$$Q_3 = 62.5 + \frac{140.25 - 135}{28} \times 1 = 62.688$$

Hence, Bowley's coefficient, $S_B = \frac{Q_1 - Q_3 - 2Q_2}{Q_3 - Q_1} = 0.048$

The distribution is positively skewed (right-skewed) because S_B is positive ($B > 0$). This suggests that the tail on the right side of the distribution is longer or heavier.

5.4.2.3 Kelly's Measure

By comparing the values of specific percentiles (usually the 10th, 50th, and 90th percentiles) or deciles (10th, 20th,..., 90th percentiles) of the dataset, Kelly's measure of skewness allows one to quantify the degree of skewness in a distribution. To evaluate the skewness of the data, it specifically compares the difference between the median (50th percentile) and the average of the 10th and 90th percentiles (also known as deciles).

Based on Percentiles

Skewness as per Kelly's Measure

$$S_K = \frac{P_{90} + P_{10} + 2P_{50}}{2}$$

Where P_{90}, P_{10}, P_{50} are the 90th, 50th and 10th Percentiles.
Coefficient of Skewness as per Kelly's Measure

$$S_{KL} = \frac{90th \text{ } percentile + 10th \text{ } Percentile + 2 \times 50th \text{ } Percentile}{90th \text{ } percentile - 10th \text{ } Percentile}$$

Based on Deciles

$$S_K = \frac{D_9 + D_1 + 2D_5}{D_9 - D_1}$$

where, D_9, D_5 and D_1 are 9th, 5th and 1st Decile.

Coefficient of Kelly's Measure

> - If SKL is positive, it indicates positive skewness, meaning the distribution has a longer right tail.
> - If SKL is negative, it indicates negative skewness, meaning the distribution has a longer left tail.
> - If SKL is close to zero, it suggests that the distribution is approximately symmetric.

5.4.2.3.1 Computation of Kelly's Measure of Skewness in case of Individual Series

Example: Calculate Kelly's Coefficient of Skewness for the following data: 5, 7, 8, 9, 10, 12, 15, 16, 18, 20.

Solution: Find the 10th Percentile

To find the 10th percentile, we need to rank the data in ascending order and find the value below which 10% of the data falls. In this dataset, the 10th percentile corresponds to the value at position 1 since 10% of 10 data points is 1. So, the 10th percentile is 5.

$$P_{10} = 5$$

Find the 50th Percentile (Median)

Since there are 10 data points, the median is the average of the 5th and 6th values when sorted in ascending order

$$Median = \frac{10 + 12}{2} = \frac{22}{2} = 11$$

$$P_{50} = 11$$

Find the 90th Percentile

To find the 90th percentile, you need to identify the value below which 90% of the data falls. In this dataset, the 90th percentile corresponds to the value at position 9 since 90% of 10 data points is 9. So, the 90th percentile is 18.

$$P_{90} = 18$$

Substitute the values in the formula.

$$S_{KL} = \frac{P_{90} + P_{10} + 2P_{50}}{P_{90} - P_{10}} = \frac{18 + 5 - 2 \times 11}{18 - 5} = 0.07$$

Since the number is positive, Kelly's Skewness Coefficient shows that the distribution has a tiny positive skewness, indicating it has a larger right tail. This suggests that there may be some data points on the right side of the distribution that are substantially larger compared to the bulk of data points.

5.5 Magnitude of Skewness

> ➢ An approximately symmetric distribution is indicated by a skewness value close to 0 (between -0.5 and 0.5);
> ➢ Strong left skewness is suggested by a significantly negative skewness value (below -1)
> ➢ Strong right skewness is suggested by a significantly positive skewness value (above 1).
> ➢ If a distribution's mean, median, and mode all have the same value, then the distribution is not skew.
> ➢ Skewness does not exist if the sum of the frequencies on either side of the mode is equal.
> ➢ Skewness does not exist if the first and third quartiles are the same distance from the median. The greater the difference in these values, the greater the skewness. Likewise, if the first and ninth deciles and the first and 99 percentiles are equally spaced from the median.
> ➢ There is no asymmetry if the sums of the positive and negative deviations from the mean, median, or mode are equal. Additionally, if a data graph shows

5.6 Moments

The rth moment about mean of a distribution, denoted by μ_r, is given by

$$\mu_r = \frac{1}{N} \sum_{i-1}^{n} f_i (X_i - \bar{X})^r$$

Thus, r^{th} moment about mean is the mean of the rth power of deviations of observations from their arithmetic mean. In particular

$$\text{if } r = 0, \text{ we have } \mu_0 = \frac{1}{N} \sum_{i-1}^{n} f_i (X_i - \bar{X})^0 = 1$$

$$\text{if } r = 1, \text{ we have } \mu_1 = \frac{1}{N} \sum_{i-1}^{n} f_i (X_i - \bar{X})^1 = 0$$

$$\text{if } r = 2, \text{ we have } \mu_2 = \frac{1}{N} \sum_{i-1}^{n} f_i (X_i - \bar{X})^2 = \sigma^2$$

$$\text{if } r = 3, \text{ we have } \mu_3 = \frac{1}{N} \sum_{i-1}^{n} f_i (X_i - \bar{X})^3 \text{ and so on}$$

These moments are also known as central moments.

In addition to the above, we can define raw moments as moments about any arbitrary mean.

Let A denote an arbitrary mean, then r^{th} moment about A is defined as

$$\mu_r' = \frac{1}{N} \sum_{i-1}^{n} f_i(X_i - A)^r , r = 0,1,2,3 \ldots$$

When A = 0, we get various moments about origin.

5.6.1 Moment Measure of Skewness

The moment measure of skewness is based on the property that, for a symmetrical distribution, all odd ordered central moments are equal to zero. We note that $\mu_0 = 0$, for every distribution, therefore, the lowest order moment that can provide an absolute measure of skewness is μ_3. Further, a coefficient of skewness, independent of the units of measurement, is given by

$$\alpha_3 = \frac{\mu_3}{\sigma^3} = \pm\sqrt{\beta_1} = \gamma_1$$

β_1 and γ_1 are defined as the first beta and first gamma coefficients respectively. Note that β_2 is a measure of kurtosis as you will come to know in the below Section.

Very often, the skewness is measured in terms of $\beta_1 = \frac{\mu_3^2}{\mu_2^3}$, where the sign of skewness is determined by the sign of μ_3

5.6.1.1 Computations of Moment Measure of Skewness

Example: Compute the Moment coefficient of skewness (β_1) from the following data.

Marks Obtained:	0-10	10-20	20-30	30-40	40-50	50-60	60-70
Frequency	6	12	22	24	16	12	8

Solution: The second moment μ_2 is equal to the variance (σ^2) and its positive square root is equal to standard deviation (σ).

$$\mu_2 = \frac{1}{N} \sum_{i-1}^{n} f_i(X_i - \bar{X})^2 = \sigma^2$$

Table for the computations of mean, s.d. and μ_3.

Marks Obtained:	Frequency (f)	Mid values(X)	$u = \dfrac{X-35}{10}$	fu		fu^2	fu^3
0-10	6	5	-3	-18		54	-162
10-20	12	15	-2	-24		48	-96
20-30	22	25	-1	-22		22	-22
30-40	24	35	0	0		0	0
40-50	16	55	1	16		16	16
50-60	12	55	2	24		48	96
60-70	8	65	3	24		72	216
Total	100			0		260	48

$$\mu_2 = \frac{1}{N}\sum_{i-1}^{n} f_i(X_i - \bar{X})^2 = \sigma^2$$

Since $\sum fu = 0$, the mean of the distribution is 35, then

$$\mu_2 = \frac{260}{100} \times 100 = 260 \; and$$

$$s.d(\sigma) = \sqrt{260} = 16.12$$

Also, $\mu_3 = \frac{48}{100} \times 1000 = 480$

Then, $\beta_1 = \frac{(48)^2}{260^3} = 0.01$

Since the sign of μ_3 is positive and β_1 is small, the distribution is slightly positively skewed.

If the mean of a distribution is not a convenient figure like 35, as in the above example, the computation of various central moments may become a cumbersome task. Alternatively, we can first compute raw moments and then convert them into central moments by using the equations obtained below.

5.6.2 Conversion of Raw Moments into Central Moments

We can write

$$\mu_r = \frac{1}{N}\sum_{i-1}^{n} f_i (X_i - \bar{X})^r = \frac{1}{N}\sum_{i-1}^{n} f_i [(X_i - A) - (\bar{X} - A)]^r = \frac{1}{N}\sum_{i-1}^{n} f_i [(X_i - A) - \mu_1']^r$$

Expanding the term within brackets by binomial theorem, we get

$$= \frac{1}{N}\sum_{i-1}^{n} f_i [r_{C_0}((X_i - A)^r \mu_1'^0 - r_{C_1}(X_i - A)^{r-1}\mu_1' + r_{C_2}(X_i - A)^{r-2}\mu_1'^2 - \dots]$$

$$= \frac{1}{N}\sum_{i=1}^{n} f_i (X_i - A)^r \mu_1'^0 - r_{C_1}\frac{1}{N}\sum_{i=1}^{n} f_i (X_i - A)^{r-1}\mu_1'^2 + r_{C_2}\sum_{i=1}^{n} f_i (X_i - A)^r \mu_1'^2 - \dots$$

From the above, we can write

$$\mu_r = \mu_2' - r_{C_1}\mu_{r-1}'\mu_2' + r_{C_2}\mu_{r-2}'\mu_1'^2 - r_{C_3}r_{C_2}\mu_{r-3}'\mu_1'^2 + \dots$$

In particular, taking r = 2, 3, 4, etc., we get

$$\mu_2 = \mu_2' - 2_{C_1}\mu_r'^2 + 2_{C_2}\mu_0'\mu_1'^2 = \mu_2' - \mu_1'^2 \ (\mu_0' = 1)$$

$$\mu_3 = \mu_3' - 3\mu_2'\mu_0' + 3\mu_3' - \mu_2'^2 = \mu_3' - 3\mu_2'\mu_1' + 2\mu_1'^3$$

$$\mu_4 = \mu_4' - 4\mu_3'\mu_1' + 6\mu_2'\mu_1'^2 - 4\mu_1'^4 + \mu_1'^4 = \mu_4' - 4\mu_3'\mu_1' + 6\mu_2'\mu_1'^2 - 3\mu_1'^4$$

5.6.2.1 Computation of the first four moments about mean

Example: Compute the first four moments about mean from the following data.

Class Intervals :	0 – 10	10 – 20	20 – 30	30 – 40
Frequency (f) :	1	3	3	2

Solution:

Table for computations of raw moments (Take A = 25)

Class Intervals	f	Mid-value	$u = \dfrac{X - 25}{10}$	fu	fu^2	fu^3	fu^4
0 –10	1	5	-2	-2	4	-8	16
10-20	3	15	-1	-3	3	-3	3

20-30	3	25	0	0	0	0	0
30-40	2	35	1	2	2	2	2
Total				-3	9	-9	21

From the above table, we can write

$$\mu_1' = \frac{-3 \times 10}{10} = -3$$

$$\mu_2' = \frac{9 \times 10^2}{10} = 90$$

$$\mu_3' = \frac{9 \times 10^3}{10} = -900$$

$$\mu_4' = \frac{21 \times 10^4}{10} = 2100$$

Moments about Mean

By definition,

$$\mu_r = 0$$

$$\mu_2 = 90 - 9 = 81$$

$$\mu_3 = -900 - 3 \times 90 \times (-3) + 2 \times (-3)^3 = -900 + 810 - 54 = -144$$

$$\mu_4 = 2100 - 4 \times (-900) \times (-3)^3 - 3 \times (-3)^4$$

$$= 21000 - 10800 + 4860 - 243 = 14817$$

5.7 Concept and measures of Kurtosis

5.7.1 Concept of Kurtosis: One statistical metric used to characterize a feature of a dataset is kurtosis. Data that is regularly distributed typically takes the shape of a bell when plotted on a graph. We call this the bell curve. On either side of the curve, the tails are often the depicted data that deviate the most from the mean. Kurtosis shows the amount of information in the tails.

- Kurtosis describes the "fatness" of the tails found in probability distributions.
- Kurtosis risk is a measurement of how often an investment's price moves dramatically.
- A curve's kurtosis characteristic tells you how much kurtosis risk there is for the investment you're evaluating.

Kurtosis is a metric that quantifies the total weight of a distribution's tails in relation to the mean, or center of the distribution curve. For instance, a histogram graphing a set of roughly normal data reveals a bell peak, with the majority of the data falling within three standard deviations (plus or minus) of the mean. On the other hand, the tails of the normal bell-shaped distribution extend beyond the three standard deviations when there is substantial kurtosis (Nagar, A. L. et al., 1983).

A distribution's shape can also be measured by kurtosis, which is a measure of the relative peakedness of its frequency curve, while skewness measures the distribution's lack of symmetry. As illustrated in given Fig., different frequency curves can be classified into three groups based on the shape of their peaks: Leptokurtic, Mesokurtic, and Platykurtic (Yule, G U. et al., 1991).

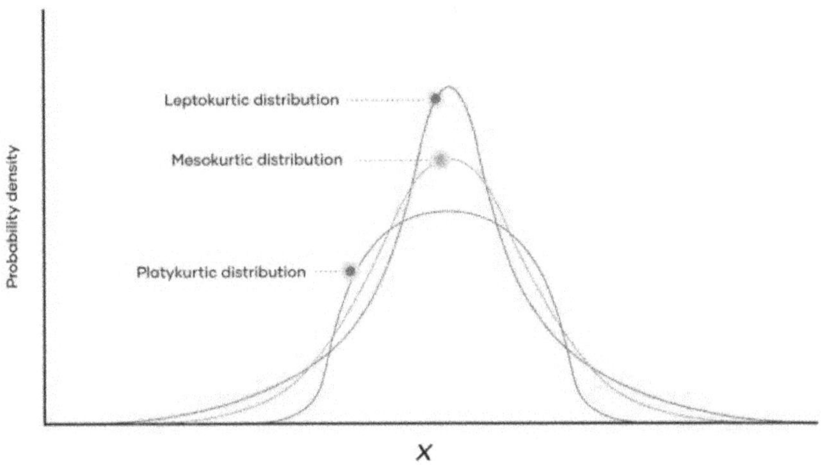

Fig.5.2: Platykurtic Curve, Mesokurtic Curve and Leptokurtic Curve

5.7.2 Types of kurtosis

Mesokurtic, leptokurtic, and platykurtic kurtosis are the three types that can be seen in these data sets. A normal distribution curve is used as a comparison point for all kurtosis measurements.

5.7.2.1 Mesokurtic (Kurtosis = 3.0)

The mesokurtic distribution is the first type of kurtosis. The extreme value feature of this distribution is comparable to that of a normal distribution since its kurtosis is comparable to that of the latter. As a result, a mesokurtic distribution typically indicates a modest degree of risk in stocks.

5.7.2.2 Leptokurtic (Kurtosis > 3.0)

The second type is the leptokurtic distribution, which is characterized by greater kurtosis than a mesokurtic distribution and manifests as a curve with long tails (outliers). The leptokurtic distribution's "skinniness" is a result of the outliers, which cause the histogram graph's horizontal axis to stretch, resulting in the bulk of the data appearing in a narrow ("skinny") vertical range. A stock with a leptokurtic distribution typically shows a high degree of risk but also the potential for higher returns because the stock has historically shown significant price movements.

5.7.2.3 Platykurtic (Kurtosis < 3.0)

The platykurtic distribution is the last distribution type. Short tails (fewer outliers) characterize these distributions. Due to the rarity of large price swings in the past, platykurtic distributions have proven to be more stable than other curves. This corresponds to a risk level that is below moderate.

5.7.3 Measures of Kurtosis

5.7.3.1 Karl Pearson's Measures of Kurtosis

For calculating the kurtosis, the second and fourth central moments of variable are used. For this, following formula given by Karl Pearson is used:

$$\beta_2 = \frac{\mu_4}{\mu_2^2}$$

or
$$\gamma_2 = \beta_2 - 3$$

where, μ_2 = Second order central moment of distribution

μ_4 = Fourth order central moment of distribution

Description:

1. If $\beta_2 = 3$ or $\gamma_2 = 0$, then curve is said to be mesokurtic;

2. If $\beta_2 < 3$ or $\gamma_2 < 0$, then curve is said to be platykurtic;

3. If $\beta_2 > 3$ or $\gamma_2 > 0$, then curve is said to be leptokurtic;

5.7.3.2 Kelly's Measure of Kurtosis

Kelly has given a measure of kurtosis based on percentiles. The formula is given by

$$\beta_2 = \frac{P_{75} - P_{25}}{P_{90} - P_{10}}$$

where, P_{75}, P_{25}, P_{90}, and P_{10} are 75th, 25th, 90th and 10th percentiles of dispersion respectively.

If $\beta_2 > 0.26315$, then the distribution is platykurtic.

If $\beta_2 < 0.26315$, then the distribution is leptokurtic

5.7.3.3 Computation of coefficient of skewness and kurtosis

Example: First four moments about mean of a distribution are 0, 2.5, 0.7 and 18.75. Find coefficient of skewness and kurtosis.

Solution: we have $\mu_1 = 0$, $\mu_2 = 2.5$, $\mu_3 = 0.7$, and $\mu_4 = 18.75$

Therefore the formula of Skewness, $\beta_1 = \dfrac{\mu_3^2}{\mu_2^3} = \dfrac{(0.7)^2}{(2.5)^3} = 0.031$

And $\qquad\qquad\qquad$ Kurtosis, $\beta_2 = \dfrac{\mu_4}{\mu_2^2} = \dfrac{18.75}{(2.5)^2} = \dfrac{18.75}{6.25} = 3$

As β_2 is equal to 3, so the curve is mesokurtic.

Example: The first four raw moments of a distribution are 2, 136, 320, and 40,000. Find out coefficients of skewness and kurtosis.

Solution: we have given $\mu_1' = 2$, $\mu_2' = 136$, $\mu_3' = 320$, and $\mu_4' = 40,000$

First, we have to calculate the first four central moments

$$\mu_1 = 0$$

$$\mu_2 = \mu_2' - {\mu_1'}^2 = 136 - (2)^2 = 132$$

$$\mu_3 = \mu_3' - 3\mu_2'\mu_1' + 2{\mu_1'}^3$$

$$= 320 - 3 \times 132 \times 2 + 2(2)^3$$

$$= 320 - 792 + 16 = -456$$

$$\mu_4 = \mu_4' - 4\mu_3'\mu_1' + 6\mu_2'{\mu_1'}^2 - 3{\mu_1'}^4$$

$$= 40000 - 4 \times 2 \times 320 + 6 \times 2^2 \times 136 - 3 \times 2^4$$

$$= 40000 - 2560 + 3264 - 48 = 40656$$

Therefore the formula of Skewness, $\beta_1 = \dfrac{\mu_3^2}{\mu_2^3} = \dfrac{(-456)^2}{(132)^3} = 0.0904$

And $\qquad\qquad\qquad$ Kurtosis, $\beta_2 = \dfrac{\mu_4}{\mu_2^2} = \dfrac{40656}{(132)^2} = 2.333$

Summary

One important statistical metric for characterizing a distribution's asymmetry is skewness. It indicates the degree and direction of skewness and can be either positive, negative, or zero. This asymmetry is quantified by skewness measures like the moment coefficient and Pearson's coefficients (Mansfield, E., 1991). Making educated decisions and comprehending the data distribution require the ability to interpret skewness. You have studied skeweness and kurtosis measurements in this unit. You can use these two ideas to obtain a sense of how a distribution's frequency curve looks. Kurtosis measures the relative peakedness of a frequency curve's top, while skewness measures the absence of symmetry.

Although they both measure the form of a probability distribution statistically, kurtosis and skewness concentrate on different elements. A distribution's tailedness is measured by kurtosis. A distribution's asymmetry is measured by its skewness (Yule, G U. et al., 1991).

Chapter 6: Correlation

6.1 Concept of Correlation: Prior statistical methods (such dispersion and central tendency) are only capable of analyzing a particular variable or statistical analysis. The term Univariate Distribution refers to this kind of statistical study when just one variable is used. In the actual world, however, there are cases where distributions contain two variables, such as information on income and expenses, pricing and demand, height and weight, etc. Bivariate distribution is the name given to the distribution that has two variables. The discovery of connections between two or more statistical series is required. A statistical method for establishing the connection between two variables is correlation (Peters, W.S. et al., 1968).

6.1.1 What is Correlation?

A statistical metric called correlation indicates how closely two variables are related to one another. It measures how strongly and in which direction the variables have a linear relationship. A statistical tool that helps in the study of the relationship between two variables is known as Correlation. It also helps in understanding the economic behaviour of the variables. Generally, it is denoted by the symbol 'r' and ranges from -1 to 1 (Peters, W.S. et al., 1968).

The two variables are said to be correlated if a change in one causes a corresponding change in the other variable. For example, A change in the price of a commodity leads to a change in the quantity demanded. An increase in employment levels increases the output. When income increases, consumption increases as well (Stevenson, W.J. 1978).

6.1.2 Definitions of Correlation

According to L.R. Connor, "If two or more quantities vary in sympathy so that movements in one tend to be accompanied by corresponding movements in others, then they are said to be correlated."

In the words of Croxton and Cowden, "When the relationship is of a quantitative nature, the appropriate statistical tool for discovering and measuring the relationship and expressing it in a brief formula is known as correlation."

According to A.M. Tuttle, "Correlation is an analysis of covariation between two or more variables."

6.1.3 Significance of Correlation

> ➢ It aids in figuring out how closely the two variables in a single figure are correlated.
> ➢ It identifies important and crucial variables and facilitates comprehension of economic behavior.
> ➢ It is possible to estimate the value of one variable by utilizing the value of the other when two variables are correlated. The regression coefficients are used for this.

> Correlation aids in decision-making in the business sector. Making predictions with the use of the correlation lowers uncertainty. The reason for this is because correlation-based predictions are most likely accurate and near to reality.

6.2 Scatter Diagram

The values of two variables, X and Y, as well as their relationship to one another, are displayed in a scatter diagram. The vertical axis displays the values of variable Y, while the horizontal axis displays the values of variable X.

One of the variables is later designated as an independent variable and the other as a dependent variable when the regression model is applied. The independent variable X is thought to have some influence or effect on the dependent variable Y in regression (Stevenson, W.J. 1978).. The statistical consideration of correlation methods does not include any evidence of causality or direction of influence, and they are symmetric with respect to the two variables. The example below shows a scatter diagram. The correlation coefficient is then calculated using the same example.

6.3 Types of Correlation

The scatter plot illustrates how the two characteristics or variables are correlated. It shows the degree of correlation between the two variables. To observe the relationship between the two variables, there are three possible scenarios:

6.3.1 Correlation can be classified based on various categories: Based on the direction of change in the value of two variables, correlation can be classified as:

6.3.1.1 Positive correlation: occurs when the values of the two variables move in the same direction, meaning that as one variable's value increases or decreases, the other variable's value also increases or decreases.
For example, Relationship between the price and supply, income and expenditure, height and weight, etc.

6.3.1.2 Negative correlation: When the values of the two variables move in the opposite directions, such that a rise or fall in one variable is followed by a rise or fall in the other, this is known as negative correlation. **For example,** the relationship between the price and demand, temperature and sale of woollen garments, etc.

6.3.1.3 No correlation: It occurs when the two variables have no relationship or linear dependence.

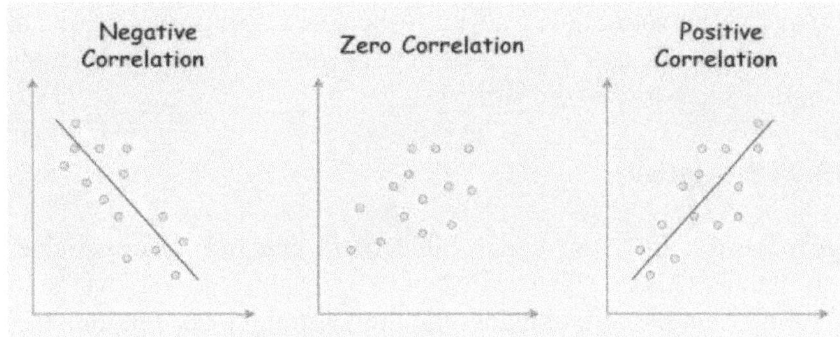

Fig: 6.1: Three types of correlation

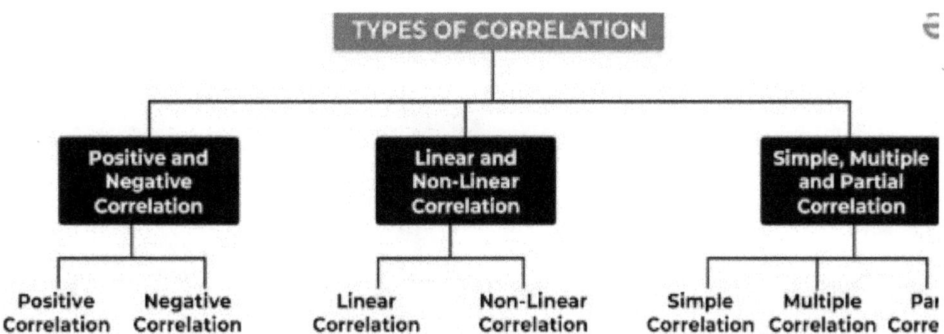

Fig: 6.2 Different Types of correlation

6.3.2 Based on the ratio of variations between the variables, correlation can be classified as:

6.3.2.1 Linear Correlation: Linear correlation occurs when a change in one variable causes a constant change in the amount of another variable. When two variables change in the same proportion, this phrase is used (Draper, N. et al., 1966). On graph paper, the relationship between two variables that fluctuate in a predetermined proportion will be represented as a straight line. Consequently, it implies a linear relationship.

Example:

X	10	15	20	25	30
Y	10	20	30	40	50

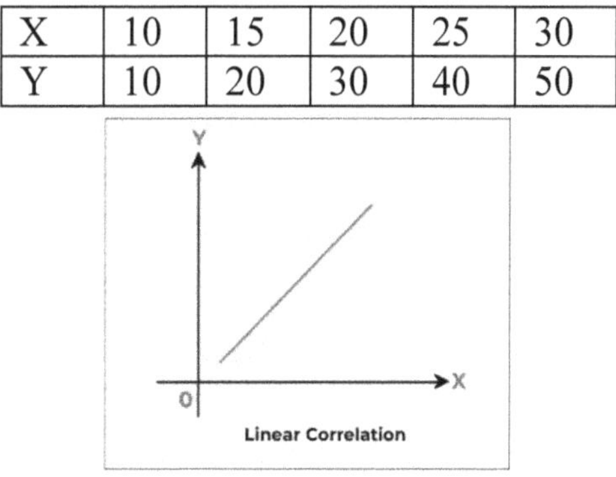

Fig:6.3 linear correlation

In the above graph, for every change in the variable X by 5 units there is a change of 10 units in variable Y. The ratio of change of variables X and Y in the above schedule is 1:2 and it remains the same, thus there is a linear relationship between the variables.

6.3.2.2 Non-Linear (Curvilinear) Correlation:

When there is no constant change in the amount of one variable due to a change in another variable, it is known as a Non-Linear Correlation. This term is used when two variables do not change in the same ratio (Draper, N. et al., 1966). This shows that it does not form a straight-line relationship. For example, the production of grains would not necessarily increase even if the use of fertilizers is doubled.

Example:

X (Fertilizer)	10	20	30	40	50
Y(Production of grains)	7	12	19	25	35

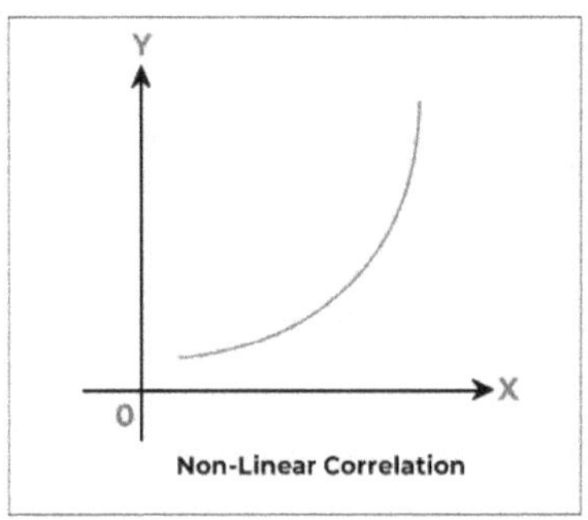

Fig:6.4 Nonlinear correlation

In the above schedule, there is no specific relationship between the variables. Even though both change in the same direction i.e. both are increasing, they change in different proportions. The ratio of change of variables X and Y in the above schedule is not the same, thus there is a non-linear relationship between the variables.

6.3.3 Based on the number of variables involved, correlation can be classified as:

6.3.3.1 Simple Correlation: This suggests that only the two variables are being studied. For instance, the connection between price and money supply and the relationship between price and demand (Box, G.E.P., et al., 1976).

6.3.3.2 Partial Correlation: This refers to the analysis of two variables while holding other factors constant. For instance, a number of variables, such as rainfall, manure quality, seed quality, etc., affect wheat productivity. However, there is only a limited association between wheat and seed quality when rainfall and manure are held constant.

6.3.3.3 Multiple Correlation: This refers to the simultaneous examination of three or more variables. All of the independent and dependent variables are examined at the same time. For instance, the connection between rainfall, seed quality, and wheat yield.

6.4 Degree of Correlation

There are three categories of correlation. When two variables change proportionately, there is perfect correlation (Box, G.E.P., et al., 1976). If both rise or drop simultaneously, it is positive (+1); if they move in opposing directions, it is negative (-1). When the correlation coefficient is zero, it indicates that there is no relationship between the variables. With values ranging from -1 to +1, limited correlation lies between perfect and zero correlation (Srivastava, U.K et al., 1987). If changes happen in the same direction, it's positive; if they happen in the other direction, it's negative. There are three classifications for the degree of correlation: low (0 to 0.25), moderate (0.25 to 0.75), and high (0.75 to 1).

The degree of correlation is measured through the coefficient of correlation. The degree of correlation for the given variables can be expressed in the following ways:

Table for Degree of Correlation

Degree of Correlation	Positive Correlation	Negative Correlation
Perfect Correlation	+1	+1
Very High Degree of Correlation	+0.9	+0.9
Fairly High Degree of Correlation	Between +0.75 and +0.9	Between +0.75 and +0.9
Moderate Degree of Correlation	Between +0.25 and +0.75	Between +0.25 and +0.75
Low Degree of Correlation	Between) and +0.25	Between) and +0.25
Zero/No Correlation (uncorrelated)	0	0

6.5 What is Correlation Coefficient Formula?

To ascertain the strength of a relationship between the data, the correlation coefficient approach is employed. A number between 1 and -1 is produced by the correlation coefficient technique. Where by,

- A significant negative association is indicated by a value of -1.
- 1 denotes a high degree of favorable associations.
- Zero suggests that there is no link at all.

Correlation shows the relation between two variables. Correlation coefficient shows the measure of correlation. To compare two datasets, we use the correlation formulas (Box, G.E.P., et al., 1976).

6.4.1 Comprehending the Correlation Coefficient

- A correlation coefficient of -1 indicates that for every positive gain in one variable, there is a corresponding reduction of a certain amount. For example, a tank's gas level drops in precise proportion to speed.

- A correlation coefficient of one indicates that for every positive increase in one variable, a fixed proportion of others increases as well. For example, the shoe's size increases in perfect proportion to the length of the foot.

- A correlation value of zero indicates that there is neither a positive nor a negative rise for each increment. Simply said, the two are unrelated.

6.5 Types of Correlation Coefficient Formula

6.5.1 Karl Pearson Correlation Coefficient Formula

The British biometrician Karl Pearson (1867–1936) developed the coefficient of correlation, which quantifies the strength or degree of a linear relationship between two variables. For linear dependency between the data sets, the Karl Pearson Correlation coefficient is the most widely used formula. The coefficient's value falls between -1 and +1 (Srivastava, U.K et al., 1987). The data is regarded as unrelated when the coefficient drops to zero. Conversely, a number of +1 indicates a positive correlation between the data, while a value of -1 indicates a negative correlation (Edwards, B. 1980).

If X and Y are two random variables then correlation coefficient between X and Y is denoted by r and defined as

$$r_{xy} = Corr(x, y) = \frac{Cov(x, y)}{S_x S_y} \ldots\ldots\ldots (1)$$

Corr(x, y) is indication of correlation coefficient between two variables X and Y.

Where, $Cov(x, y)$ the covariance between X and Y which is defined as:

$$Cov(x, y) = \frac{1}{n} \sum_{i=1}^{n} (x_i - \bar{x})(y_i - \bar{y})$$

and $Var(x)$ the variance of X, is defined as:

$$Var(x) = \frac{1}{n} \sum_{i=1}^{n} (x_i - \bar{x})^2$$

Similarly,

$Var(y)$ the variance of Y is defined by

$$Var(x) = \frac{1}{n} \sum_{i=1}^{n} (y_i - \bar{y})^2$$

where, n is number of paired observations. Then, the correlation coefficient "r" may be defined as:

$$r = Corr(x,y) = \frac{\frac{1}{n}\sum_{i=1}^{n}(x_i - \bar{x})(y_i - \bar{y})}{\sqrt{\frac{1}{n}\sum_{i=1}^{n}(x_i - \bar{x})^2 \cdot \frac{1}{n}\sum_{i=1}^{n}(y_i - \bar{y})^2}} \quad \ldots\ldots\ldots (2)$$

Karl Pearson's correlation coefficient r is also called product moment correlation coefficient. Expression in equation (2) can be simplified in various forms. Some of them are

$$r = \frac{n(\sum xy) - (\sum x)(\sum y)}{\sqrt{[n\sum x^2 - (\sum x)^2][n\sum y^2 - (\sum y)^2]}} \quad \ldots\ldots\ldots\ldots (3)$$

Where n = Quantity of Information

$\sum x$ = Total of the First Variable Value

$\sum y$ = Total of the Second Variable Value

$\sum xy$ = Sum of the Product of first & Second Value

$\sum x^2$ = Sum of the Squares of the First Value

$\sum y^2$ = Sum of the Squares of the Second Value

6.5.2 Linear Correlation Coefficient Formula

The formula for the linear correlation coefficient is given by;

$$r_{xy} = \frac{n(\sum_{i=1}^{n} x_i y_i) - (\sum_{i=1}^{n} x_i)(\sum_{i=1}^{n} y_i)}{\sqrt{[n\sum_{i=1}^{n} x_i^2 - (\sum_{i=1}^{n} x_i)^2]\left[[n\sum_{i=1}^{n} y_i^2 - (\sum_{i=1}^{n} y_i)^2]\right]}} \quad \ldots\ldots\ldots (4)$$

6.5.2.1 Computation of Correlation Coefficient

Example: Find the correlation coefficient between advertisement expenditure and profit for the following data:

Advertisement expenditure	30	44	45	43	34	44
Profit	56	55	60	64	62	63

Solution: To find out the correlation coefficient between advertisement expenditure and profit, we have Karl Pearson's formula in many forms [(1), (2), (3), (4)] and any of them can be used. All these forms provide the same result. Let us take the form of equation (2) to solve our problem which is

$$r = Corr(x,y) = \frac{\frac{1}{n}\sum_{i=1}^{n}(x_i - \bar{x})(y_i - \bar{y})}{\sqrt{\frac{1}{n}\sum_{i=1}^{n}(x_i - \bar{x})^2 \cdot \frac{1}{n}\sum_{i=1}^{n}(y_i - \bar{y})^2}} \quad \ldots \ldots \ldots (2)$$

To find out the correlation coefficient by above formula, we require the values of $\sum_{i=1}^{n}(x_i - \bar{x})(y_i - \bar{y})$, $\sum_{i=1}^{n}(x_i - \bar{x})^2$, $\frac{1}{n}\sum_{i=1}^{n}(y_i - \bar{y})^2$ which are obtained by the following table:

Table for the calculation of Correlation Coefficient.

x	y	$x_i - \bar{x}$	$(x_i - \bar{x})^2$	$y_i - \bar{y}$	$(y_i - \bar{y})^2$	$(x_i - \bar{x})(y_i - \bar{y})$
30	56	−10	100	−4	16	40
44	55	4	16	−5	25	−20
45	60	5	25	0	0	0
43	64	3	9	4	16	12
34	62	−6	36	2	4	−12
44	63	4	16	3	9	12
$\sum x_i = 240$	$\sum y_i = 360$	$\sum(x_i - \bar{x}) = 0$	$\sum(x_i - \bar{x})^2 = 202$	$\sum(y_i - \bar{y}) = 0$	$\sum(y_i - \bar{y})^2 = 70$	$\sum(x_i - \bar{x})(y_i - \bar{y}) = 32$

Substituting in the above formula we have the correlation coefficient

$$r = Corr(x,y) = \frac{\frac{1}{n}\sum_{i=1}^{n}(x_i - \bar{x})(y_i - \bar{y})}{\sqrt{\frac{1}{n}\sum_{i=1}^{n}(x_i - \bar{x})^2 \cdot \frac{1}{n}\sum_{i=1}^{n}(y_i - \bar{y})^2}} = \frac{32}{\sqrt{202 \times 70}} = \frac{32}{118.91} = 0.27$$

As a result, there is a 0.27 link between advertising spending and profit. This suggests that there is a positive link between advertising spending and profit, meaning that as advertising spending rises or falls, profit also rises or falls. It is a week positive correlation coefficient because it falls between 0.25 and 0.5.

Example 2: Calculate Karl Pearson's coefficient of correlation between price and demand for the following data.

Price	17	18	19	20	22	24	26	28	30
Demand	40	38	35	30	28	25	22	21	20

Solution: In Example 1, we used formula given in equation (2) in which deviations were taken from mean. When means of x and y are whole number, deviations from mean makes calculation easy. Since, in Example 1, means x and y were whole number we preferred formula given in equation (2). When means are not whole numbers calculation by formula given in equation (2) becomes cumbersome and we prefer any formula given in equation (3) or (4). Since here means of x and y are not whole number, so we are preferring formula (4)

$$r_{xy} = \frac{n(\sum_{i=1}^{n} x_i y_i) - (\sum_{i=1}^{n} x_i)(\sum_{i=1}^{n} y_i)}{\sqrt{[n \sum_{i=1}^{n} x_i^2 - (\sum_{i=1}^{n} x_i)^2]\left[n \sum_{i=1}^{n} y_i^2 - (\sum_{i=1}^{n} y_i)^2\right]}}$$

Let us denote price by the variable X and demand by variable Y. To find the correlation coefficient between price i.e.X and demand Y using formula given in equation (4), we need to calculate, $\sum_{i=1}^{n} x_i$,$\sum_{i=1}^{n} y_i$, $\sum_{i=1}^{n} x_i y_i$, $\sum x_i^2$ and $\sum y_i^2$ which are being obtained in the following table:

Table for the calculation of Correlation Coefficient.

X	y	x^2	y^2	xy
17	40	289	1600	680
18	38	324	1444	684
19	35	361	1225	665
20	30	400	900	600
22	28	484	784	616
24	25	576	625	600
26	22	676	484	572
28	21	784	441	588
30	20	900	400	600
$\sum x = 204$	$\sum y = 259$	$\sum x^2 = 4794$	$\sum y^2 = 7903$	$\sum xy = 5605$

$$r_{xy} = \frac{n(\sum_{i=1}^{n} x_i y_i) - (\sum_{i=1}^{n} x_i)(\sum_{i=1}^{n} y_i)}{\sqrt{[n \sum_{i=1}^{n} x_i^2 - (\sum_{i=1}^{n} x_i)^2]\left[n \sum_{i=1}^{n} y_i^2 - (\sum_{i=1}^{n} y_i)^2\right]}}$$

$$r = \frac{(9 \times 5605)\,(204)(259)}{\sqrt{\{(9 \times 4794) - (204 \times 204)\}\{(9 \times 7903) - (259 \times 259)}}$$

$$r = \frac{50445 - 52836}{\sqrt{(43146 - 41616) \times (71127 - 67081)}}$$

$$r = \frac{-2391}{\sqrt{1530 \times 4046}}$$

$$r = \frac{-2391}{2488.0474}$$

$$r = -0.96$$

6.5.3 Sample Correlation Coefficient Formula

Sample Correlation Coefficient Formula is added below:

$$r_{xy} = \frac{Cov(x,y)}{S_x S_y} = \frac{\sum xy}{\sqrt{\sum x^2 \sum y^2}}$$

$Cov(x,y)$ is Covariance of Sample

S_x and S_y are Standard Deviations of Sample

6.5.3.1 Computation of Sample Correlation Coefficient

Example: The data of advertisement expenditure (X) and Sales (Y) of a company for the 10-year period shown in Table 1, we proceed to determine the correlation coefficient between these variables:

X	50	50	50	40	30	20	20	15	10	5
Y	700	650	600	500	450	400	300	250	210	200

Solution: we have to find out the sample correlation coefficient by using the formula is given below. First we have to find out the mean of X and Mean of Y

$$r_{xy} = \frac{\sum xy}{\sqrt{\sum x^2 \sum y^2}}$$

Table for the calculation of Sample Correlation Coefficient.

X	Y	$x = X - \bar{X}$	$y = Y - \bar{Y}$	x^2	y^2	xy
50	700	21	274	441	75076	
50	650	21	224	441	50176	
50	600	21	174	441	30276	
40	500	11	74	121	5476	
30	450	1	24	1	576	24
20	400	-9	-26	81	676	234
20	300	-9	-126	81	15876	1134
15	250	-14	-176	196	30976	2464
10	210	-19	-216	361	46656	4104
5	200	-24	-226	376	51076	5424
290	4260	0	0	2740	306840	28310

$$\bar{X} = \frac{\sum X_i}{N} = \frac{290}{10} = 29$$

$$\bar{Y} = \frac{\sum Y_i}{N} = \frac{4260}{10} = 426$$

$$r_{xy} = \frac{\sum xy}{\sqrt{\sum x^2 \sum y^2}} = \frac{28310}{\sqrt{2740 \times 306840}} = 0.976$$

There is a strong correlation between variables X and Y, as indicated by the value of r (= 0.976). Regarding this specific issue, it suggests that raising advertising spending is probably going to result in more sales.

6.5.4 Population Correlation Coefficient Formula

Population Correlation Coefficient Formula is added below:

$$\rho_{xy} = \frac{\sigma_{xy}}{\sigma_x \sigma_y}$$

where,

σ_x and σ_y are Populatin Standard Deviation

σ_{xy} is Population Covariance

6.5.5 Spearman's Rank Correlation

A statistical indicator of the direction and intensity of a monotonic relationship between two continuous variables is Spearman's Rank Correlation. As a result, they rank or arrange these qualities according to their preferences. It can have values ranging from -1 to +1 and is represented by the symbol "rho" (ρ). The two variables have a positive link when the rho value is positive, and a negative relationship when the rho value is negative. There is no correlation between the two variables when the rho value is 0.

The nonparametric Spearman's Correlation Coefficient, denoted by ρ, quantifies the degree and direction of the relationship between two ranking variables. It establishes if a relationship between two continuous or ordered variables has a monotonic component, or to what extent a relationship is monotonic.

A monotonic relationship is "less restrictive" than a linear one. If we already know that the relationship between the two variables is not monotonic, then pursuing Spearman's correlation to ascertain the strength and direction of a monotonic relationship will be pointless, even if monotonicity is not a criterion of the correlation.

Spearman's Rank Correlation Formula

$$\rho = 1 - \frac{6 \sum d_i^2}{n(n^2 - 1)}$$

where n is the number of data points of the two variables and di is the difference in the ranks of the ith element of each random variable considered. The Spearman correlation coefficient, ρ, can take values from +1 to -1.

- A ρ of +1 indicates a perfect association of ranks
- A ρ of zero indicates no association between ranks and
- ρ of -1 indicates a perfect negative association of ranks.

The closer ρ is to zero, the weaker the association between the ranks.

6.5.5.1 Computation of Spearman's Rank Correlation

Suppose the ranks obtained by a set of ten students in a Mathematics test (variable X) and a Physics test (variable Y) are as shown below:

Rank for X	1	2	3	4	5	6	7	8	9	10
Rank for Y	3	1	4	2	6	9	8	10	5	7

Solution: To determine the rank correlation, rs we can organise computations as shown in below Table

Table for the calculation of Spearman's Rank Correlation

Rank for X(Math)	Rank for Y(Physis)	$d = Y - X$	d^2
1	3	2	4
2	1	-1	1
3	4	1	1
4	2	-2	4
5	6	1	1
6	9	3	9
7	8	1	1
8	10	2	4
9	5	-4	16
10	7	-3	9
			$\sum d^2 = 50$

$$\rho = 1 - \frac{6 \sum d_i^2}{n(n^2 - 1)} = 1 - \frac{6 \times 50}{10(10^2 - 1)} = 1 - 0.303 = 0.697$$

We can thus say that there is a high degree of correlation between the performance in Mathematics and Physics.

Example: The scores for nine students in English and Science are as follows:

English: 35, 23, 47, 17, 10, 43, 9, 6, 28

Science: 30, 33, 45, 23, 8, 49, 12, 4, 31

Compute the student's ranks in the two subjects and compute the Spearman rank correlation.

Solution: First find the ranks for each individual subject. If you want to rank by hand, order the scores from greatest to smallest; assign the rank 1 to the highest score, 2 to the next highest and so on: Then Add a third column, d, to your data. The d is the difference between ranks. For example, the first student's English rank is 3 and Science rank is 5, so the difference is 2 points. In a fourth column, square your d values then we get the values in the table below.

Table for the calculation of Spearman's Rank Correlation

English(Marks)	Science(Marks)	Rank r_1	Rankr_2	d	d^2
35	30	3	5	2	4
23	33	5	3	2	4
47	45	1	2	1	1
17	23	6	6	0	0
10	8	7	8	1	1
43	49	2	1	1	1
9	12	8	7	1	1
6	4	9	9	0	0
28	31	4	4	0	0
					$\sum d^2 = 12$

$$\rho = 1 - \frac{6 \sum d_i^2}{n(n^2 - 1)} = 1 - \frac{6 \times 12}{9(9^2 - 1)} = 1 - \frac{72}{720} = 1 - 0.1 = 0.9$$

We can thus say that there is a high degree of correlation between the performance in English and Science as the value of spearman rank correlation (ρ) is 0.9.

6.6 Assumptions for Correlation Coefficient

1. The Linearity Presumption: The correlation coefficient requires that the variables be linearly connected. The scatter diagram illustrates the variables' linearity (Draper, N. et al., 1966).

2. The Presence of Normalcy: The two variables being examined ought to be distributed normally. Neither a positive nor negative skew should be present.

3. Belief in a Cause-and-Effect Connection: A cause-and-effect relationship should exist between the two variables, like in the case of children's heights and weights, the supply and demand for goods, etc. The correlation coefficient ought to be zero in the absence of a cause-and-effect relationship between variables. It is referred to as spurious correlation or chance correlation if it is not zero. For instance, the correlation coefficient between:

1. A person's weight and income over time; and

2. A state's rainfall and literacy over time.

6.7 Properties of Correlation Coefficient

1. The correlation coefficient ranges between -1 and +1.
2. The correlation coefficient remains unchanged under transformations involving a change of origin and scale.

3. If two variables, X and Y, are independent, their correlation coefficient is zero, i.e., $Cov(X, Y) = 0$.

6.8 Summary/Conclusion

The idea of correlation, or the relationship between two variables, has been covered in this section. Although a scatter plot of the variables can indicate a relationship between the two, the Pearson correlation coefficient, or r, quantifies this relationship. The values of the correlation coefficient r can range from -1 to 1 (Srivastava, U.K et al., 1987). Whether the association is inverse (-ve) or direct (+ve) is indicated by the sign. Perfect association is shown by a numerical value of r equal to unity, whereas no association is indicated by a value of zero. The correlation coefficient's significance tests have been explained. For data with rankings, Spearman's rank correlation is described. It has been emphasized how correlation can be used to find pertinent variables for factor analysis, regression, and time series forecasting (Makridakis, S. et al., 1978).

Chapter 7: Regression Analysis

Concept of Regression:

"Regression" comes from the word "regress," derived from the Latin word "regressus," which means "to go back" (to something). So, regression is the technique that helps you "to go back" from a jumbled, difficult-to-understand set of data to a simpler, more meaningful model. There are frequently two or more variables that are intrinsically connected in situations, and it could be vital to investigate the nature of their relationship. The statistical method of regression analysis is used to model and examine the relationship between two or more variables. For instance, let's say that the operating temperature of a chemical process has an impact on the product's yield. It is possible to create a model that represents yield as a function of temperature using regression analysis. With this model, yield at a specific temperature level can be predicted. It can be applied to process control or optimization as well.

7.1 What is Regression Analysis?
Regression Analysis is a supervised learning analysis where supervised learning is the analyzing or predicting the data based on the previously available data or past data. For supervised learning, we have both train data and test data. Regression analysis is one of the statistical methods for the analysis and prediction of the data. Regression analysis is used for predictive data or quantitative or numerical data.
A statistical method for assessing the type and strength of a relationship between a dependent variable (often represented by Y) and a group of independent variables (often referred to as independent variables) is regression, which looks for a mathematical relationship between a collection of random variables that are assumed to predict Y. The dependent variable is the one whose value is affected or that has to be anticipated, while the independent variable is the one that affects the values or is utilized to make predictions. in the analysis of regression. The dependent variable is sometimes referred to as the regressed or explained variable, and the regressor, predictor, or explanatory variable.

Definition: Regression analysis is a mathematical measure of the average relationship between two or more variables in terms of the original units of the data.

- Regression is a statistical technique that relates a dependent variable to one or more independent variables.
- A regression model is able to show whether changes observed in the dependent variable are associated with changes in one or more of the independent variables.
- It does this by essentially determining a best-fit line and seeing how the data is dispersed around this line.
- Regression helps economists and financial analysts in things ranging from asset valuation to making predictions.
- For regression results to be properly interpreted, several assumptions about the data and the model itself must hold.

There are various versions of regression analysis, including nonlinear, multiple linear, and linear. Multiple linear and basic linear models are the most widely used. For increasingly complex data sets where there is a nonlinear relationship between the independent and dependent variables, nonlinear regression analysis is frequently utilized.

7.1.1 Regression Formula

Regression comes in various forms, such as nonlinear, multiple linear, and linear. The most popular models are simple linear and multiple linear. For increasingly complicated data sets having nonlinear relationships between the independent and dependent variables, nonlinear regression analysis is frequently employed.

The general form of regression is:
Simple Linear Regression: $y = a + bx + \varepsilon$
Where,
Y – Dependent variable
X – Independent (explanatory) variable
a – Intercept
b – Slope
ϵ – Residual (error)

7.1.2 Importance of Regression Analysis

- **Prediction:** Forecast future trends or outcomes.
- **Understanding Relationships**: Identify how variables interact and influence each other.
- **Decision-Making**: Inform strategies by evaluating the impact of factors.
- **Hypothesis Testing**: Test theoretical relationships and validate models.
- **Risk Analysis**: Assess variables contributing to risks in business or finance.

7.2 Lines of Regression: whether there is a relationship between the variables in a bivariate distribution. The scatter diagram's points will be seen to cluster around a curve known as the "curve of regression." if a straight line represents the curve. There is linear regression between e variables, and it is referred to as the line of regression. Regression is considered curvilinear otherwise.

The line that provides the best estimate of one variable's value for any given value of the other variable is known as the line of regression. Accordingly, the line of regression, which is derived using the least squares principles, is the line of "best fit".

Let us suppose that in the bivariate distribution $(X_i, Y_i), i = 1,2,3 \dots n$; Y is dependent variable and X is independent variable.
Let the line of regression of Y on X be $Y = a + bX$
According to the principle of ·least squares. the normal equations for estimating a and b are,

$$\sum y_i = na + b \sum x_i \dots\dots (1)$$

$$\sum x_i y_i = a \sum x_i + b \sum x_i^2 \dots\dots (2)$$

Dividing (1) by n, we get

$$\bar{y} = a + b\bar{x} \dots\dots\dots (3)$$

Thus the line of regression of Y on X passes through the point $(\bar{x}, \bar{y})$.
Now

$$\mu_{11} = Cov(X,Y) = \frac{1}{n}\sum x_i y_i - \bar{x}\bar{y} \Rightarrow \frac{1}{n}\sum x_i y_i = \mu_{11} + \bar{x}\bar{y} \dots\dots (4)$$

Also $\sigma_X^2 = \frac{1}{n}\sum x_i^2 - \bar{x}^2 = \frac{1}{n}\sum x_i^2 + \bar{x}^2 \dots\dots\dots (5)$

Dividing 2 by n and use 4 and 5

$$\mu_{11} + \bar{x}\bar{y} = a\bar{x} + b(\sigma_X^2 + \bar{x}^2) \dots\dots (6)$$

Multiplying 3 by $\bar{x}$ and then subtracting it from 6, we get

$$\mu_{11} = b\sigma_X^2 \Rightarrow b = \frac{\mu_{11}}{\sigma_X^2} \dots\dots\dots (7)$$

Since ' b' is the slope of the line of regression of Yon X and since the line of regression passes
through the point (x , y), its equation is

$$Y - \bar{y} = b(X - \bar{x}) = \frac{\mu_{11}}{\sigma_X^2}(X - \bar{x}) \dots\dots\dots\dots (8)$$

$$\Rightarrow (Y - \bar{y}) = r\frac{\sigma_Y}{\sigma_X}(X - \bar{x}) \dots\dots\dots\dots (9)$$

Starting with the equation X $=$ A $+$ BY and proceeding similarly or by simply interchanging the
variables X and Y in (8) and (9), the equation of the line of regression of X on Y becomes

$$(X - \bar{x}) = \frac{\mu_{11}}{\sigma_Y^2}(Y - \bar{y}) \dots\dots\dots (10)$$

$$(X - \bar{x}) = r\frac{\sigma_X}{\sigma_Y}(Y - \bar{y}) \dots\dots (11)$$

7.2.1 Regression Curve: The regression function of Yon X is the conditional mean E(Y I X $=$ x)
for a continuous distribution is called the regression function. The graph of this function of x is

known as the regression curve of Yon X, or occasionally the regression curve for the mean of Y. The y coordinate of the centre of mass of the little bivariate probability mass in the infinitesimal vertical strip enclosed by x and x'+dx is represented geometrically by the regression function. Similarly, the regression function of X on Y is E (X I Y $=$ y) and the graph of this function of y is called the regression curve (of the mean) of X on Y. In case a regression curve' is a straight line, the corresponding regression is said to be linear. If one of the regressions is linear, it d~s not howev.er follow that the other is also linear.

7.3 Regression Coefficients: 'b', the slope of the line of regression of Y on X is also called the coefficient of regression of Y on X. It represents the increment in the value of dependent variable Y corresponding to a unit change in the value of independent variable X. More precisely, we write,

$$b_{YX} = \text{Regression coefficient of Y on X} = \frac{\mu_{11}}{\sigma_X^2} = r\frac{\sigma_Y}{\sigma_X}$$

Similarly. the coefficient of regression of X on Y indicates the change in the value of variable X corresponding to a unit change in the value of variable Y and is given by

$$b_{XY} = \text{Regression coefficient of X on Y} = \frac{\mu_{11}}{\sigma_Y^2} = r\frac{\sigma_X}{\sigma_Y}$$

7.3.1 Properties of Regression Coefficient

Some of the important properties of regression coefficients are listed below:

- We denote the regression coefficients by 'b'.
- Regression coefficients are represented as original unit of data.
- We represent the regression coefficients of y on x as b_{YX}, and of x on y as b_{XY}.
- If one of the regression coefficients is greater than 1, then the other is less than 1.
- Regression coefficients are dependent on the change of scale. The value of the coefficients changes when x and y are multiplied by any constants.
- Arithmetic mean of both the regression coefficients is greater than or equal to the coefficient of correlation.
- Geometric mean between the two regression coefficients is equal to the coefficient of correlation.
- If b_{YX} is positive then, b_{XY} is also positive and vice versa.

Property 1: Geometric mean of the regression coefficients is correlation coefficient.

Description: If regression coefficient of y on x is b_{YX} and regression coefficient of x on y is b_{XY} then geometric mean of b_{YX} and b_{XY} is correlation coefficient i.e. $\sqrt{b_{XY} \times b_{YX}} = r$

Proof: If regression coefficient of y on x is b_{YX} and regression coefficient of x on y is b_{XY} then geometric mean of b_{YX} and b_{XY}, then

$$b_{YX} \times b_{XY} = r\frac{\sigma_Y}{\sigma_X} \times r\frac{\sigma_X}{\sigma_Y}$$

$$\Rightarrow b_{YX} \times b_{XY} = r^2$$

$$\Rightarrow \pm\sqrt{b_{YX} \times b_{XY}} = r$$

It shows that geometric mean of regression coefficients is correlation coefficient.

Property 2: If one of the regression coefficients is greater than one, then other must be less than one.

Description: If b_{YX} is greater than one then b_{XY} b must be less than one.

Proof: Let b_{YX}, the regression coefficient of y on x is greater than one i.e.

$$b_{YX} > 1$$

$$\frac{1}{b_{YX}} < 1$$

We know that

$$r^2 \leq 1 \Rightarrow b_{YX} \times b_{XY} \leq 1 \qquad \text{(from Property 1)}$$

$$\Rightarrow b_{XY} \leq \frac{1}{b_{YX}} < 1$$

Thus if b_{YX} is greater than the one then b_{XY} is less than one.

Property 3: Arithmetic mean of the regression coefficients is greater than the correlation coefficient i.e $\frac{1}{2}b_{YX} \times b_{XY} \geq r$, subject to the condition $r > 0$.

Proof: Suppose that arithmetic mean of regression coefficients is greater than correlation coefficient thus,

$$\frac{1}{2}b_{YX} \times b_{XY} \geq r$$

$$\Rightarrow (b_{YX} \times b_{XY}) \geq r$$

$$\Rightarrow (b_{YX} \times b_{XY}) \geq 2(\pm\sqrt{(b_{YX} \times b_{XY})}\,\ldots\ldots\ldots(from\ Property\ 1)$$

Therefore, $\Rightarrow (b_{YX} \times b_{XY}) \geq 2(\pm\sqrt{(b_{YX}} \times \sqrt{b_{XY})} \geq 0$

$$\Rightarrow (\sqrt{(b_{YX}} \pm \sqrt{b_{XY})})^2 \geq 0$$

which is always true since the square of a real quantity is always positive. Thus, $\frac{1}{2} b_{YX} \times b_{XY} \geq r$, i.e. arithmetic mean of regression coefficients is greater than correlation coefficient.

Let us do some problems related to regression coefficients.

7.3.2 Computation of Regression Analysis

Example: Calculate the two regression equations of X on Y and Y on X from the data given below, taking deviations from a actual means of X and Y.

Price(X)	10	12	13	12	16	15
Amount(Y)	40	38	43	45	37	43

Estimate the likely demand when the price is Rs.20.

Solution:

Table for the calculation of Regression Analysis

X	$x = (X - 13)$	x^2	Y	$y = (Y - 41)$	y^2	xy
10	-3	9	40	-1	1	3
12	-1	1	38	-3	9	3
13	0	0	43	2	4	0
12	-1	1	45	4	16	-4
16	3	9	37	-4	16	-12
15	2	4	43	2	4	4
$\sum X = 78$	$\sum x = 0$	$\sum x^2 = 24$	$\sum Y = 246$	$\sum y = 0$	$\sum y^2 = 50$	$\sum xy = -6$

$$\bar{X} = \frac{\sum X}{N} = \frac{78}{6} = 13$$

$$\bar{Y} = \frac{\sum Y}{N} = \frac{246}{6} = 41$$

(i) Regression equation of X on Y using equation (11), we get

$$(X - \bar{x}) = r \frac{\sigma_X}{\sigma_Y} (Y - \bar{y})$$

$$b_{XY} = r \frac{\sigma_X}{\sigma_Y} = \frac{\sum xy}{\sum y^2} = \frac{-6}{50} = -0.12$$

$$(X - 13) = -0.12(Y - 41)$$

$$(X - 13) = -0.12Y + 4.92$$

$$X = -0.12Y + 17.92$$

(ii) Regression Equation of Y on X using equation (9), we get

$$(Y - \bar{y}) = r\frac{\sigma_Y}{\sigma_X}(X - \bar{x})$$

$$b_{YX} = r\frac{\sigma_Y}{\sigma_X} = \frac{\sum xy}{\sum x^2} = \frac{-6}{24} = -0.25$$

$$(Y - 41) = -0.25(X - 13)$$

$$(Y - 41) = -0.25X + 3.25$$

$$Y = -0.25X + 44.25$$

When X is 20, Y will be

$$Y = -0.25(20) + 44.25$$

$$= -5 + 44.25$$

$$= 39.25$$

$Y = 39.25$ (when the price is Rs. 20, the likely demand is 39.25)

Example: Calculate the regression coefficient and obtain the lines of regression for the following data.

X	1	2	3	4	5	6	7
Y	9	8	10	12	11	13	14

Solution:

Table for the calculation of Regression Analysis

X	Y	X^2	Y^2	XY
1	9	1	81	9
2	8	4	64	16
3	10	9	100	30
4	12	16	144	48
5	11	25	121	55
6	13	36	169	78
7	14	49	196	98
$\sum X = 28$	$\sum Y = 77$	$\sum X^2 = 140$	$\sum Y^2 = 875$	$\sum XY = 334$

$$\bar{X} = \frac{\sum X}{N} = \frac{28}{7} = 4$$

$$\bar{Y} = \frac{\sum Y}{N} = \frac{77}{7} = 11$$

Regression coefficient of X on Y

$$b_{XY} = \text{Regression coefficient of X on Y} = \frac{N\sum XY - (\sum X)(\sum Y)}{N\sum Y^2 - (\sum Y)^2}$$

$$= \frac{7(334) - (28)(77)}{7(875) - (77)^2}$$

$$= \frac{2338 - 2156}{6125 - 5929}$$

$$= \frac{182}{196}$$

$$b_{XY} = 0.929$$

(i)   Regression equation of X on Y

$$(X - \bar{X}) = b_{XY}(Y - \bar{Y})$$
$$(X - 4) = 0.929(Y - 11)$$
$$(X - 4) = 0.929Y - 10.219$$

Therefore the regression equation of X on Y is $X = 0.929 - 6.219$

(ii)   Regression coefficient of Y on X

$$b_{YX} = \text{Regression coefficient of Y on X} = \frac{N\sum XY - (\sum X)(\sum Y)}{N\sum X^2 - (\sum X)^2}$$

$$= \frac{7(334) - (28)(77)}{7(140) - (28)^2}$$

$$= \frac{2338 - 2156}{980 - 784}$$

$$= \frac{182}{196}$$

$$b_{YX} = 0.929$$

(iii)   Regression equation of Y on X

$$(Y - \bar{Y}) = b_{YX}(X - \bar{X})$$

$$(Y - 11) = 0.929(X - 4)$$
$$Y = 0.929X - 3.716 + 11$$
$$Y = 0.929X + 7.284$$

The regression equation of Y on X is Y= 0.929X + 7.284

Example: Find the means of X and Y variables and the coefficient of correlation between them from the following two regression equations:

$$2Y - X - 50 = 0$$
$$3Y - 2X - 10 = 0$$

Solution: We are given

$$2Y - X - 50 = 0 \ldots \ldots (1)$$
$$3Y - 2X - 10 = 0 \ldots \ldots \ldots (2)$$

Solving equation (1) and (2)

We get $\quad Y = 90$

Putting the value of Y in equation (1)

We get $\quad X = 130$

Here $\bar{X} = 130 \ and \ \bar{Y} = 90$

Calculating correlation coefficient

Let us assume equation (1) be the regression equation of Y on X

$$2Y = X + 50$$

$$Y = \frac{1}{2}X + 25 \ therefore \ b_{YX} = \frac{1}{2}$$

Clearly equation (2) would be treated as regression equation of X on Y

$$3Y - 2X - 10 = 0$$

$$2X = 3Y - 10$$

$$X = \frac{3}{2}Y - 5 \ therefore \ b_{XY} = \frac{3}{2}$$

The correlation coefficient $r = \pm\sqrt{b_{XY} \times b_{YX}} = \sqrt{\frac{1}{2} \times \frac{3}{2}} = 0.866$

Example: There are two series of index numbers P for price index and S for stock of the commodity. The mean and standard deviation of P are 100 and 8 and of S are 103 and 4 respectively. The correlation coefficient between the two series is 0.4. With these data obtain the regression lines of P on S and S on P.

Solution: Let us consider X for price P and Y for stock S. Then the mean and SD for P is considered as X-Bar = 100 and $\sigma_x = 8$ respectively and the mean and SD of S is considered as Y-Bar =103 and $\sigma_y = 4$. The correlation coefficient between the series is $r(X, Y) = 0.4$

Let the regression line X on Y be

$$(X - \bar{x}) = r \frac{\sigma_X}{\sigma_Y} (Y - \bar{y})$$

$$(X - 100) = (0.4) \frac{8}{4} (Y - 103)$$

$$(X - 100) = (0.8)(Y - 103)$$

$$X - 0.8Y - 17.6 = 0 \; or \; X = 0.8Y + 17.6$$

The regression line Y on X be

$$(Y - \bar{y}) = r \frac{\sigma_Y}{\sigma_X} (X - \bar{x})$$

$$(Y - 103) = (0.4) \frac{4}{\sigma_X^2} (X - \bar{x})$$

$$(Y - 103) = 0.2(X - 100)$$

$$Y = 0.2X + 83 \; or \; 0.2X - Y + 83 = 0$$

7.3 Types of regression analysis

Regression analysis comes in different forms, such as nonlinear, multiple linear, and linear. The most popular models are simple linear and multiple linear. For more complicated data sets, nonlinear regression analysis is employed. There is a nonlinear link between the dependent and independent variables.

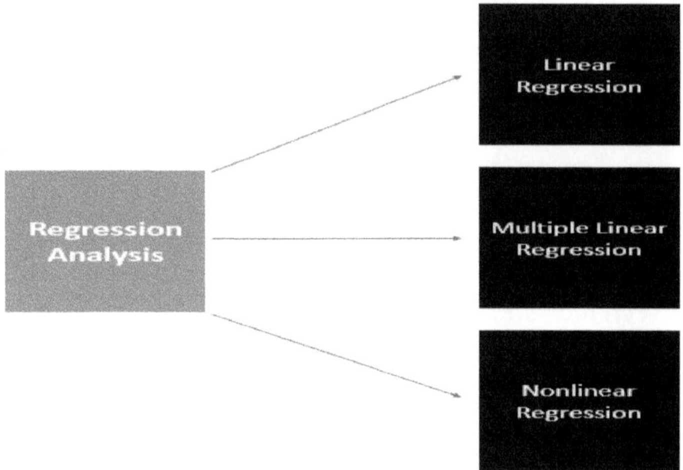

Fig 7.1 Types of Regression Analysis

The two fundamental forms of regression are simple linear regression and multivariate linear regression. To predict the result of the dependent variable Y, multiple linear regression employs two or more independent variables. Simple linear regression, on the other hand, describes or forecasts the result of the dependent variable Y using a single independent variable.

7.3.1 Simple Linear Regression
It is a fundamental form of linear regression analysis. Only one dependent variable and one independent variable are present in this straightforward linear regression. Only one predictor is used in this linear regression model. The linear relationship between the independent and dependent variables is provided by this linear regression model. Regression analysis that is frequently employed is simple linear regression. Market analysis, financial research, and weather forecasting are the main applications for this straightforward linear regression approach. It can be utilized for result prediction, model efficiency enhancement, and taking the appropriate steps to avoid model errors.

The simple linear regression model's mathematical formula is displayed below.

$$y = a + bx + \varepsilon$$

Where, y is a dependent variable
x is a independent variable
a, b are the regression coefficients

a is also called as slope b is the intercept of the linear equation as the equation of the simple linear regression is like the slope intecept form of the line , where slope intercept form
$y = mx + c$. The slope of the equation may be positive or negative (i.e, value of a may be positive or negative).

7.3.1.1 Example of Linear Regression

A regression line may show a linear relationship that is positive, negative, or nonexistent. Regarding a Basic Linear Regression: $y = a + bx + \varepsilon$

Situation 1: If b = line slope = 0: No relationship exists: The graphed line in simple linear regression is flat, not sloping. There is no link between the two variables.

Situation 2: If b = line slope = +ve: With its lower end at the graph's y-intercept (axis) and its upper end extending upward into the graph field, away from the x-intercept (axis), the regression line slopes upward. A positive linear relationship exists between the two variables, meaning that when one increases in value, the other does too.

Situation 3: b = slope of line = -ve: With its top end at the graph's y-intercept (axis) and its lower end continuing downward into the graph field, toward the x-intercept (axis), the regression line slopes downward. The two variables have a negative linear connection, meaning that when one rises in value, the other falls.

7.3.1.2 Assumptions for Linear Models in Regression Analysis

Six basic presumptions form the basis of linear regression analysis:

- The slope and the intercept of the dependent and independent variables exhibit a linear connection.
- There is no randomness in the independent variable.
- The residual, or mistake, has a value of zero.
- For every observation, the residual's (error's) value remains constant.
- There is no correlation between the residual (error) value and all observations.
- The normal distribution is followed by the residual (error) values.

7.3.2 Multiple linear regression analysis

A dependent variable and two or more independent variables are related, as shown by multiple linear regression analysis. The hyperplane in multidimensional space is one way to depict multiple linear regression. Additionally, it is a regression analysis of the linear kind. The main distinction between it and linear regression is the number of independent variables. Real estate, finance, business, public health, and other domains all make use of multilinear regression analysis.

The multiple linear regression mathematical equation is displayed below.

$$y = a + bX_1 + cX_2 + dX_3 + \varepsilon$$

Where:

Y – Dependent variable

$X_1,\ X_2,\ X_3$ – Independent (explanatory) variables

a – Intercept

b, c, d – Slopes, ε– Residual (error)

The requirements for multiple linear regression are identical to those for the simple linear model. However, because multiple linear analysis involves several independent variables, the model must also meet the following additional requirements:

Non-collinearity: There should be little to no connection between independent variables. It will be challenging to determine the actual links between the independent and dependent variables if there is a high degree of correlation between the independent variables

7.4 Difference Between Correlation and Regression

The difference between correlation and regression are as follows:

1. As the name suggests, "regression" describes how an independent variable is quantitatively related to the dependent variable, while "correlation" establishes the connection or co-relationship between the variables.
2. There is no difference in the correlation between the independent and dependent values.However, the independent and dependent variables are separate in regression.
3. Finding a numerical or quantitative value that captures the relationship between the values is the main objective of correlation. But the primary objective of regression is to use the values of a fixed variable to determine the values of a random variable.
4. The establishment of a relationship between the two variables is facilitated by correlation. Determining the value of a variable that depends on another value is made easier by regression.

7.5 Application of Regression analysis

- In finance, regression is used to calculate a stock's beta, or the volatility of returns relative to the market as a whole.
- Multiple regression can be used to forecast a company's financial statements by examining how future sales or expenses may be impacted by shifts in certain expectations or market forces.
- Regression is used for forecasting and prediction. This has a direct connection to machine learning.
- Regression is also utilized in a variety of industries, including manufacturing, marketing, and medicine. Understanding projected price, product income, and the effectiveness of marketing efforts are all beneficial. It aids in assessing the correlation between the factors that determine a higher engine's efficiency. It helps in forecasting different drug combinations and creating generic medications for ailments.
- Based on these results, regression assists a credit card firm in understanding a number of things, including a customer's likelihood of credit default, anticipated consumer behavior, credit balance forecast, and so forth. The business then offers particular EMI choices while reducing default rates among high-risk clients.

- Regression is utilized in risk analysis, predictive analysis, business optimization, and decision-making processes.

7.6 Summary

This chapter discusses a statistical technique for examining the relationship between variables, specifically the changes in a dependent variable with respect to an independent variable, is regression. Regression coefficients, which measure the direction and strength of this link, are computed when lines of regression have been obtained (Kutner, M. H., N et al., 2004). Certain characteristics of these coefficients include their invariance to changes in origin but not scale. Regression lines are crucial for forecasting the dependent variable from the independent variable's given values (Hastie, T., et al., 2009). Correlation evaluates the direction and intensity of the linear association between variables without inferring causation, whereas regression focuses on creating a predictive relationship.

References

Agresti, A. (2018). *Statistical Methods for the Social Sciences*. Pearson.

Asthana H.S, and Bhushan, B.(2007) Statistics for Social Sciences (with SPSS Applications). Prentice Hall of India

B.L.Aggrawal (2009). Basic Statistics. New Age International Publisher, Delhi.

Efron, B., & Tibshirani, R. J. (1994). *An Introduction to the Bootstrap*. Chapman & Hall.

Freedman, D., Pisani, R., & Purves, R. (2007). *Statistics*. W. W. Norton & Company.

Gelman, A., Carlin, J. B., Stern, H. S., Dunson, D. B., Vehtari, A., & Rubin, D. B. (2013). *Bayesian Data Analysis*. Chapman & Hall/CRC.

Gupta, S.C.(1990) Fundamentals of Statistics. Himalaya Publishing House, Mumba.

Hastie, T., Tibshirani, R., & Friedman, J. (2009). *The Elements of Statistical Learning: Data Mining, Inference, and Prediction*. Springer.

Hively, W., Patterson, H. L., & Page, S. H. (1968). A" universe-defined" system of arithmetic achievement tests. Journal of educational measurement, 5(4), 275-290.

Stigler, S. M. (1986). *The History of Statistics: The Measurement of Uncertainty before 1900*. Harvard University Press.

Tukey, J. W. (1977). *Exploratory Data Analysis*. Addison-Wesley.

Winters R, Winters A, Amedee RG. Statistics: A brief overview Ochsner J. 2010;10:213–6

Ziliak, S. T., & McCloskey, D. N. (2008). *The Cult of Statistical Significance: How the Standard Error Costs Us Jobs, Justice, and Lives*. University of Michigan Press.

Dawson B, Trapp RG. 4th ed. New York: McGraw Hill; 2004. Basic and clinical biostatistics. Gravetter FJ, Wallnau LB. 5th ed. Belmont: Wadsworth – Thomson Learning; 2000. Statistics for the behavioral sciences

Sundaram KR, Dwivedi SN, Sreenivas V. 1st ed. New Delhi: B.I Publications Pvt Ltd; 2010. Medical statistics principles and methods.

Swinscow, T. D., & Campbell, M. J. (2003). Statistics at square one. (Indian).

McCluskey A Lalkhen AG, Statistics I: Data and correlations, CEACCP, 2007, vol. 7 (pg. 95-99)

Bland M, An Introduction to Medical Statistics, 20003rd Edn.OxfordOxford University Press

Altman DG, Practical Statistics for Medical Research, 1991LondonChapman & Hall/CRC

Rumsey D, Statistics for Dummies, 2003New Jersey Wiley Publishing Inc

SurfStat Australia (accessed 14 June 2007) http://www.anu.edu.au/nceph/surfstat/surfstat-home/surfstat.html

Elwood M, Critical Appraisal of Epidemiological Studies and Clinical Trials, 19982nd Edn.Oxford University press

Bordens, K. S., & Abbott, B. B. (2011). Research design and methods: A process approach (8 ed.). New York: McGraw-Hill.

Swinscow TD, Campbell MJ. Statistics at square one. 10thed (Indian). New Delhi: Viva Books Private Limited; 2003.

Gravetter FJ, Wallnau LB. Statistics for the behavioral sciences. 5th ed. Belmont: Wadsworth – Thomson Learning; 2000.

Sundaram KR, Dwivedi SN, Sreenivas V. Medical statistics principles and methods. 1sted. New Delhi: B.I Publications Pvt Ltd; 2010.

Petrie A, Sabin C. Medical statistics at a glance. 3rd ed. Oxford:WileyBlackwell;2009.

Norman GR, Streiner DL. Biostatistics the bare essentials. 2nd ed. Hamilton: B.C. Decker Inc; 2000. SundarRao PS, Richard J. Introduction to biostatistics and research methods. 4thed. New Delhi: Prentice Hall of India Pvt Ltd; 2006.

Glaser AN. High Yield Biostatistics. 1st Indian Ed. New Delhi:Lippincott Williams and Wilkins;2000. Dawson B, Trapp RG. Basic and Clinical Biostatistics. 4thed. New York: McGraw Hill; 2004.

Freund, J.E., & Perles, B.M. (2006). Modern Elementary Statistics. Pearson Education.

Gupta, S.P. (2014). Statistical Methods. Sultan Chand & Sons.

King, B. M., Rosopa, P. J., & Minium, E. W. (2013). Statistical reasoning in the behavioral sciences. John Wiley & Sons.

Moore, D.S., Notz, W.I., & Fligner, M.A. (2018). The Basic Practice of Statistics (8th Edition). W.H. Freeman.

Bluman, A.G. (2017). Elementary Statistics: A Step by Step Approach. McGraw Hill Education.

Tate, R. F. (1955). The theory of correlation between two continuous variables when one is dichotomized. Biometrika, 42(1/2), 205-216.

Goneppanavar U, Ali Z, Bhaskar SB, Divatia JV. Types of data, methods of collection, handling and distribution Airway. 2019;2:36–40

Kannan S, Dongare PA, Garg R, Harsoor SS. Describing and displaying numerical and categorical data Airway. 2019;2:64–70

Myles PS, Gin T. Statistical Methods for Anaesthesia and Intensive Care 20001st Oxford Butterworth Heinemann:8–10

Ali Z, Bhaskar SB. Basic statistical tools in research and data analysis Indian J Anaesth. 2016;60:662–9

Schneider A, Hommel G, Blettner M. Linear regression analysis: Part 14 of a series on evaluation of scientific publications Dtsch Arztebl Int. 2010;107:776–82

Aggarwal R, Ranganathan P. Common pitfalls in statistical analysis: Linear regression analysis Perspect Clin Res. 2017;8:100–2

Campbell MJ, Swinscow TD. Correlation and regression Statistics at Square One. 200911th

Bolch, B. W. (1968). More on unbiased estimation of the standard deviation. Amer. Statist., 22, 27.

Cureton, E. E. (1968). Unbiased estimation of the standard deviation. Amer. Statist., 22, 22.

Kothari CR, Research Methodology: Methods and Techniques, 2nd Edition, New Age International (P) Ltd, New Delhi.

Malhotra NK, Birks DF, Marketing Research an Applied Approach, 4th Edition, Prentice Hall, New Delhi.

A. M. Goon, M. K. Gupta and B. Dasgupta, Fundamentals of Statistics Vol.1, 2008, World Press Organization (P) Ltd, India.

A.K. Sharma, Text Book of Elementary Statistics, 2005, Discovery Publishing House, New Delhi.

Garrett, H.E. (1981), Statistics in Psychology and Education, (Tenth edition), Bombay, Vakils Feffer and Simons Ltd.

McBride, Dawn M. (2018). The Process of Statistical Analysis in Psychology. Sage. USA

Minium, E.W., King, B.M. & Bear. G (2001). Statistical Reasoning in Psychology and Education (3rd edition), Singapore, John Wiley & Sons, Inc.

Mohanty, B. & Misra, Santa (2016). Statistics for Behavioural and Social Sciences. Sage. New Delhi.

Kendall, M. G. and Stuart, A. (1977). The Advanced Theory of Statistics, Vol. 1. Griffin, London, England.

Pearson, E. S. and Kendall, M. G. (1970). *Studies in the History of Statistics and Probability*. Griffin, London, England. (This is a detailed history of statistical ideas with a very full list of references.)

Holtzman, W. H. (1950). The unbiased estimate of the population variance and standard deviation. *Amer. J. Psychol.*, 63, 615–617.

Markowitch, E. (1968). Minimum mean-square error estimation of the standard deviation of the normal distribution. *Amer. Statist.*, 22, 26.

Elhance, D. N. and V. lhance, 1988, Fundamentals of Statistics, Kitab Mahal, Allahabad.

Nagar, A. L. and R. K. Dass, 1983, Basic Statistics, Oxford University Press, Delhi .

Mansfield, E., 1991, Statistics for Business and Economics: Methods and Applications, W.W. Norton and Co.

Yule, G U. and M. G Kendall, 1991, An Introduction to the Theov of Statistics, Universal Books, Delhi.

Box, G.E.P., and G.M. Jenkins, 1976. Time Series Analysis, Forecasting and Control, Holden-Day: San Francisco.

Peters, W.S. and G.W: Summers, 1968. Statistical Analysis for Business Decisions, Prentice Hall: Englewood-Cliffs.

Srivastava, U.K., G.V. Shenoy and S.C. Sharma, 1987. Quantitative Techniques for Managerial Decision Making,Wiley Eastern: New Delhi.

Stevenson, W.J. 1978. Business Statistics-Concepts and Applications, Harper and Row: New York.

Draper, N. R., & Smith, H. (2014). Applied Regression Analysis. Wiley.

Field, A. (2017). Discovering Statistics Using IBM SPSS Statistics. Sage Publications.

Kutner, M. H., Nachtsheim, C. J., & Neter, J. (2004). Applied Linear Regression Models. McGraw-Hill Education.

Hastie, T., Tibshirani, R., & Friedman, J. (2009). The Elements of Statistical Learning. Springer.

Montgomery, D. C., Peck, E. A., & Vining, G. G. (2015). Introduction to Linear Regression Analysis. Wiley.